DEZINFORMATSIA...

"...describes an important and successfully exploited weapon in the Soviet war against the West..."
—*NATIONAL REVIEW*

"...an excellent new eye-opening book..."
—*TORONTO SUN*

"...an important book."
—*WASHINGTON TIMES*

"...a primer on how the Soviets go about disseminating whatever it is they want us to hear..."
—*LOS ANGELES HERALD EXAMINER*

"Most Western journalists have neither the time nor energy to approach the subject of disinformation systematically, and are uninformed about its widespread use by the Soviets...it deserves greater attention—attention it receives in this book."
—*CHRISTIAN SCIENCE MONITOR*

DEZINFORMATSIA

ACTIVE MEASURES IN SOVIET STRATEGY

RICHARD H. SHULTZ
& ROY GODSON

BERKLEY BOOKS, NEW YORK

DEZINFORMATSIA: ACTIVE MEASURES IN SOVIET STRATEGY

A Berkley Book/published by arrangement with
Pergamon Press Inc.

PRINTING HISTORY
Pergamon Press edition published 1984
Berkley edition/May 1986

ISBN: 0-425-08772-7

A BERKLEY BOOK ® TM 757,375
Berkley Books are published by The Berkley Publishing Group,
200 Madison Avenue, New York, New York 10016.
The name "BERKLEY" and the stylized "B"
with design are trademarks belonging to
Berkley Publishing Corporation.

PRINTED IN THE UNITED STATES OF AMERICA

ACKNOWLEDGMENTS

For several years, the authors have been studying and teaching about international relations, strategy, and conventional and covert instruments of statecraft. In the course of conversations about the evolution of academic courses in national security policy, Frank R. Barnett, President of the National Strategy Information Center (NSIC), postulated the need for a scholarly work incorporating information about Soviet propaganda and available knowledge regarding the Soviet use of covert instruments. He further suggested that such a volume, analyzing little-known techniques that affect everyday attitudes in the West, would be of interest and use to journalists and policy-makers as well as to teachers and interested laypersons.

For twenty years, NSIC has initiated and sponsored scholarly research and teaching in national security-related subjects. As a logical extension of that program, Mr. Barnett encouraged us to undertake this project and made available to us the facilities and support of NSIC—a nonpartisan, tax-exempt educational foundation. This enabled the authors to secure assistance from two types of specialists. First, leading academic authorities on Soviet history and foreign policy were asked to comment on the authors' research design, and later on the draft manuscript. This academic review panel consisted of Frederick C. Barghoorn (Yale), Robert Conquest (Hoover Institution on

War, Revolution and Peace), William E. Griffith (Massachusetts Institute of Technology), Uri Ra'anan (Fletcher School of Law and Diplomacy), Donald W. Treadgold (University of Washington), and Adam Ulam (Harvard). Their advice and recommendations, reflecting several academic disciplines, were invaluable.

Other experts—former and current US government specialists in Communist propaganda and Soviet "active measures"—also were extremely helpful. On their own time, they too critiqued the research design and made useful suggestions regarding various technical aspects of the study. For their generous and professional contributions, we are indebted to George Constantinides, John Dziak, William Mills, Raymond Rocca, Herbert Romerstein, and Norman Smith. The authors alone, however, assume responsibility for the facts, arguments, interpretations, and conclusions of this study.

Joyce E. Larson, Associate Editor at NSIC's New York office, did an exceptional editorial job. Her diligent attention to detail, valuable insights, and constructive criticism are deeply appreciated by the authors.

We also benefited enormously from the assistance and encouragement of Dorothy E. Nicolosi of NSIC; the editorial assistance of Georgine DiVirgilio; and the technical and research support of Jeffrey Berman, Paul Bland, Jill Fall, and Christine Thompson (all of NSIC's Washington, DC staff).

We also wish to thank Kevin Maxwell, Director of Publishing at Pergamon Press, Inc. We appreciate his enthusiasm, encouragement, and support for the continuing study of a multidimensional subject which is fully deserving of the attention he is devoting to it in this book and other projected volumes on Soviet "active measures."

PREFACE

This book contains an illuminating analysis of the techniques of Soviet overt and covert propaganda directed against the free world, and particularly against the United States. Its perusal is bound to awaken the political sleepwalkers of the Western world who are unaware or require more evidence that the sophisticated political strategy of the Soviet Union against democratic societies, which began long ago, continues today. The Kremlin has used these techniques with great skill and resourcefulness. The changing map of the world since 1917 registers the success of the global strategy of the Communist movement, aided in part by the political ignorance and innocence of the citizens of the free world.

Readers initially may have some difficulty in overcoming their sense of incredulity at what the authors report. However, as they become familiar with the documentation and reflectively assess the evidence presented, those who read this book will become convinced of the importance of its theme, and the sobriety of the subject's treatment in the hands of the authors.

For reasons that will be apparent to those who turn over even a few of its pages, a study of this book should be part of the professional training of anyone engaged in the communications industry at any political level, particularly in foreign affairs. Some public-spirited philanthropist or foundation ought to arrange to put a copy of this book into the hands of every newspaperman and newspaperwoman, and every radio and television commentator. No one unaware of the contents of this volume can understand fully the difficulties faced by the free world in its struggle for survival.

Why the concerns of this study also should interest the ordinary citizen rather than just the specialist in communications and foreign affairs is a question which may be asked. The answer is that the activities it reveals, and the analyses it contains of the Soviet apparatus for propaganda and covert techniques, bear directly on the issues of war and peace, which are inescapable for any reflective person. Although the Soviet Union is prepared to expand by military means wherever it can do so without paying too heavy a cost, its preferred strategy is to win the fruits of victory without running unnecessary risks. This it seeks to achieve by sowing confusion in the West, generating rifts and mutual distrust among the democratic powers, "Finlandizing" Western Europe, and isolating the United States.

A free nation can be weakened by its failure to understand the ideas of its enemies as well as by its failure or unwillingness to defend itself. Indeed, the latter may be a consequence of the former. Soviet leaders enjoy the advantage, granted by their closed society, of barring their subjects from hearing or reading the words broadcast and published in the free world. They also enjoy the right, extended by the free world, to send their messages and preach their doctrines beyond the borders of the USSR. The free world needs no defense against the ideas and words *per se* of Moscow and its allies. The evidence from the historical records and the arguments that can be marshaled against Communism are deadly. However, the free world does need, first, an adequate defense against the Kremlin's military power. After that, it needs an adequate defense—provided by knowledge and understanding—against Communist propaganda stratagems.

Karl Jaspers, the noted German philosopher, once said that the truth sometimes needs its own propaganda. I interpret this to mean only that the truth needs the courage to speak the truth.

That is the best defense against the systematic lie. This book attempts to defend our embattled, imperfect free society by telling the truth about a subject some would prefer to ignore. The democracies no longer can afford such ignorance. There is no guarantee that making the truth known will keep us free, but it certainly will help in the struggle to preserve our freedom.

Sidney Hook
South Wardsboro, Vermont

CONTENTS

CHAPTER I

INTRODUCTION

DISAGREEMENT CLEARLY EXISTS regarding the importance Moscow places in the utility of overt and covert propaganda and political influence techniques as instruments of foreign policy. This question continues to stimulate heated public debate in the West.

On one side are those who believe that these techniques continue to play a central role in Kremlin strategy. Recently senior American and European officials have called attention to what they believe is a major and worldwide Soviet political offensive. Many analysts share this perspective. For example, one leading scholar of Soviet foreign policy, commenting in the early 1980s on recent developments in West Germany, has observed that "Soviet propaganda, directed by the International Information Department of the Central Committee, has effectively fed intellectual ammunition and, indirectly, probably some money to the West German peace movement." While maintaining that the peace movement was "neither begun nor is it controlled by Moscow," this specialist nevertheless concludes that the Soviets currently are "more active in West German politics than at any time since 1933."[1] Others disagree. They maintain that since the Soviet Union has become a military superpower, leaders in the Kremlin no longer regard these techniques as important. This study, however, concludes that

1

propaganda and political influence techniques do in fact constitute significant instruments of Soviet foreign policy and strategy.

Even before their seizure of power, Bolshevik leaders defined international politics as a continuing state of conflict or struggle. The Soviet Union constantly has rejected the Western notion that world politics fluctuates between periods of war and peace. Soviet leaders do not regard war and politics as distinct conditions; rather, from their perspective, politics is a continual state of war carried on by a wide variety of means, sometimes including military operations. Thus, Moscow views international politics as a constant struggle. Soviet leaders employ a broad range of military and non-military measures against all adversaries. Included in this approach are all techniques deemed effective.

Soviet leaders use the term "active measures" (*aktivnyye meropriatia*) to describe an array of overt and covert techniques for influencing events and behavior in, and the actions of, foreign countries. Prior to the 1960s, the term *dezinformatsia* was used in some Soviet circles to describe these instruments. Active measures may entail influencing the policies of another government, undermining confidence in its leaders and institutions, disrupting relations between other nations, and discrediting and weakening governmental and non-governmental opponents. This frequently involves attempts to deceive the target (foreign governmental and non-governmental elites or mass audiences), and to distort the target's perceptions of reality.

Active measures may be conducted overtly through officially-sponsored foreign propaganda channels, diplomatic relations, and cultural diplomacy. Covert political techniques include the use of covert propaganda, oral and written disinformation, agents of influence, clandestine radios, and international front organizations. (As will be apparent throughout this study, these covert techniques often are interrelated and intertwined in practice.) Active measures also may involve military maneuvers or paramilitary assistance to insurgent movements and terrorist groups.

The Soviet leadership employs these overt and covert political techniques to strengthen allies and weaken opponents and to create a favorable environment for the achievement of Soviet foreign policy objectives. While other nations from time to time do the same, the Soviet Politburo both qualitatively and quantitatively uses these instruments in a very different way. In the Soviet usage, overt and covert political techniques are much more centrally coordinated and intensive. They also are systematically and routinely conducted on a worldwide scale. Soviet leaders, for example, use covert political means in most—if not all—non-Communist states to enhance dramatically their themes of overt propaganda, employing intentional misrepresentation, exaggeration, and outright falsehoods on a very large scale. These overt and covert political campaigns also can be, and frequently are, sustained over long periods of time. Few (if any) Western governments, in peacetime, emulate these activities.

In conjunction with other elements of statecraft, the Soviets closely integrate active measures into their overall strategy. As is the case with military, economic, and diplomatic instruments, the Kremlin designs and employs these measures to support Soviet strategic objectives and operations. The Soviets presumably seek to achieve enhanced global power and influence, if possible without employing military force. Active measures play a central role by weakening opponents of the USSR without the necessity of fighting.

This study demonstrates how the leaders of the Soviet Union use active measures in one of the most important areas of contemporary world politics—the North Atlantic Treaty Organization (NATO) region. Since the early days of the post-World War II period, the main targets of Soviet active measures have been the United States and the NATO alliance. Kremlin leaders consistently have sought to discredit, isolate, and separate the United States from its allies. The ongoing Soviet campaign against the modernization of NATO's intermediate-range nuclear forces (INF) is one of the most dramatic illustrations of these propositions. For some years, the Soviets have mounted a large-scale campaign of coordinated diplomatic moves, overt propaganda, and covert political action aimed at preventing such modernization.

Unfortunately, until very recently contemporary students of Soviet affairs have not sought to systematically describe and explain this aspect of Soviet behavior. There is today no scholarly study of Soviet overt and covert propaganda and political influence activities, their interrelationship, and their role in contemporary Soviet strategy. This is surprising, in view of the fact that Soviet leaders in both their doctrine and their actions emphasize the importance of these tactics, and devote extensive organizational and financial resources to them.[2]

The present study begins to fill this gap in the scholarly literature. It highlights and documents the major ways in which Moscow employs propaganda and political influence techniques in pursuit of its foreign policy and strategic objectives. The book will not attempt to assess the impact of these Soviet efforts. Clearly, however, leaders in the Kremlin believe their investment is worthwhile. They show no signs of disenchantment with these techniques and are unlikely to change their ways, at least in the near future.

After this brief introductory chapter, the main body of the study is divided into five parts. Chapter II focuses on Moscow's foreign policy perspectives and the role of active measures in Soviet strategy. It delineates the concepts, the doctrine, and the impressive organizational and financial structure which Moscow has created to conduct these activities. Chapter III examines one of the major targets of Soviet foreign propaganda efforts in the post-World War II period: Moscow's attempt to divide the West by disrupting and splitting the NATO alliance. The chapter emphasizes the overt propaganda campaign conducted by the Soviets between 1960 and 1980, with specific attention to the 1960–1962, 1967–1969, and 1976–1979 periods. To identify the major overt propaganda themes directed against the West, the weekly "International Review" column in *Pravda*, the major authoritative Soviet newspaper, has been analyzed systematically through the use of a computerized form of content analysis.

This basically quantitative approach is supplemented by a more qualitative assessment of selected articles from *New Times*, a world affairs weekly published by the International Department of the Communist Party of the Soviet Union (CPSU) and distributed worldwide in several languages.

Chapter IV demonstrates how the Soviets operate secretly to promote and enhance the effectiveness of their overt propaganda. The Kremlin of course goes to enormous lengths to hide these covert techniques. Indeed, it is not easy to detect and document these activities. Nevertheless, it is possible to demonstrate persuasively that the Soviets integrate overt propaganda with covert political techniques to multiply the effectiveness of their overall effort. The chapter examines Soviet manipulation of the propaganda disseminated by one of a number of Soviet-controlled international front organizations, the World Peace Council, and its subsidiary national Peace Councils. Additionally, the chapter describes how the Soviets used at least one major agent of influence to affect the politics of France, a key player in NATO, and how this agent—for over twenty years—secretly replayed Soviet propaganda. The chapter also focuses on Soviet forgeries, a form of disinformation, to document further the complex relationship between overt and covert Soviet techniques and the importance of these tactics to Soviet objectives.

Chapter V is composed of interviews with former Soviet bloc intelligence officers who specialized in covert political techniques in the early 1960s through the late 1970s. Their responses to a series of questions posed by the authors provide unique insights concerning the way Soviet leaders conduct these operations and the means used by Moscow to evaluate their effectiveness. Chapter VI summarizes the major findings of the study, and considers policy implications for Western strategy.

CHAPTER II

SOVIET PERSPECTIVES AND STRATEGY

FOREIGN POLICY PERSPECTIVES, STRATEGY, AND BUREAUCRACY

Soviet Foreign Policy Perspectives

Many scholars have concluded that there is a fundamental difference between the perspectives of Soviet and Western leaders on the nature of world politics, which in turn affects their approaches to foreign policy. In large part, Soviet assumptions about international relations reflect the principles of Marxism-Leninism, and have remained consistent since the establishment of the Soviet regime.

In their recent study *Soviet Foreign Policy Since World War II*, Joseph Nogee and Robert Donaldson, building on the earlier classic work of Nathan Leites, address this consistency in the Soviet understanding of and approach to world politics. "There is a complex of attitudes in Marxist-Leninist theory that characterizes the Communist's view of the political world and his relationship to it," Nogee and Donaldson write. These attitudes "rest upon the fundamental premise that all political activity . . . involves conflict," and reflect the view that "in a world of

7

differing social systems, war and conflict are the normal state of affairs."[1] (Democratic governments, on the other hand, make a sharp distinction between war and peace, and do not assume that a continual state of conflict is characteristic of international relations.) In another recent study, Adam Ulam notes that even during the period of Soviet-American "detente" in the 1970s, Moscow's approach to world politics remained basically unchanged. "As Moscow has viewed it," Ulam writes, "detente must not be allowed to limit its freedom of action or to impair the ability to play the international politics game according to its own rules . . . the USSR did not propose to purchase Western goodwill by altering its traditional policies."[2]

Ample evidence of continuing Soviet adherence to these precepts can be found in available Soviet sources, including the writing and speeches of leading Party and military officials.[3] Leonid Brezhnev, for example, announced on a number of occasions that peaceful coexistence would not entail a weakening of the world revolutionary struggle; on the contrary, the struggle would intensify and antagonisms would sharpen between the two systems. In 1973, Brezhnev stated that "the revolution, the class struggle and Marxism-Leninism cannot be abrogated by order or by agreement . . . we are fighting to ensure favorable international conditions for advancing the cause of social progress."[4] This view was reiterated by Brezhnev in 1976 at the Twenty-Fifth Congress of the CPSU:[5]

> Bourgeois politicians . . . raise a howl over the solidarity of Soviet Communists and the Soviet people with the struggle of the peoples for freedom and progress. This is either naivete or, more likely, deliberate obfuscation. . . . Peaceful coexistence . . . does not in the slightest abolish, and it cannot abolish or alter, the laws of class struggle.

Marshal A. A. Grechko similarly asserted that the Leninist perspective on conflict, war, and politics continues to underlie Soviet political-strategic concepts and related military doctrine. According to Grechko:[6]

Lenin's definition of the nature of war serves as the key to proper understanding of the socio-political content of past and present wars. . . . Lenin teaches that "war is simply a continuation of politics by other (specifically violent) means". . . . This was always the viewpoint of Marx and Engels, who examined every war as the continuation of policies and powers. . . . Soviet military science is guided . . . by the Leninist definition of the essence of war as a continuation of politics through other, specifically forcible, means.

What these statements suggest is a continuing Soviet adherence to a dynamic and dialectical view of history, which stresses that political interaction and movement are the result of conflict —conflict which almost always occurs between each historical period's principal adversaries. As one leading Soviet spokesman has observed, "rivalry, struggle, and conflict of the two opposing systems are objectively inescapable," and will continue "as long as two different socio-economic systems exist."[7] The main antagonist, according to the Soviet viewpoint, is the entity which has the capability and the will to inflict the most grievous harm. Once the main antagonist is identified, the Soviet approach requires that this entity be separated from its allies and isolated in the international system.

Therefore, as implied above by Ulam and as commentary by leading Soviet officials confirms, the worldview of the Kremlin and its approach to politics generally have remained consistent. Further examination of the extensive body of coherent and reasonably frank Soviet commentary on this subject is beyond the scope of the present study. However, attention should be drawn in this connection to a recent book by R. Judson Mitchell entitled *Ideology of a Superpower: Contemporary Soviet Doctrine on International Relations*. In this volume, Mitchell notes that while various Soviet sources identify important structural changes in the international system of the 1970s and the 1980s, the basic principles underpinning contemporary Soviet doctrine on international relations continue to reflect the consistency in approach described in the works of Nogee and Donaldson,

Ulam, Alvin Rubinstein, and other specialists on Soviet foreign policy.[8] For Moscow today, world politics remains a continual situation of conflict and war.

Doctrinal considerations, in turn, provide the broad framework or prism through which the Soviets identify foreign policy objectives, and the various elements of the Party's political-military strategy then serve these foreign policy aims. This is not meant to suggest that the influence of Soviet doctrine on Moscow's foreign policy objectives and behavior necessarily is simple and direct; quite clearly, many factors influence those officials who set foreign policy goals.[9] Nevertheless, a discernible linkage does appear to exist between the doctrinal outlook of Soviet leaders and the broad foreign policy objectives they set for the USSR.

Ample (although certainly not unanimous) support for this thesis is available in the Western literature on Soviet politics. Rubinstein, for example, explicates this relationship between doctrine and foreign policy objectives in his comments on the important distinctions between the Soviet policy of peaceful coexistence and the Western concept of detente. While peaceful coexistence originally sought "to buttress [the] essentially defensive strategy" of earlier years, by the Brezhnev period it had been "refashioned for a strong . . . imperial Soviet Union." Thus, Rubinstein explains, "implicit in peaceful coexistence are continued rivalry, endemic suspicion, and unrelenting effort to weaken the adversary in order to alter the correlation of world forces through a combination of political, economic, cultural, and ideological means."[10] By contrast, in the West (particularly in the United States), detente was widely viewed as an agreement between East and West to moderate—not accelerate—these tactics.

While the specific policies promoted by leaders in the Kremlin will reflect, of course, the situation and issues unique to a given period of time, the following broad objectives of Soviet foreign policy—both offensive and defensive—have been identified by many Western scholars.[11] (1) Preserve, enhance, and expand security in those areas under the influence of the

USSR. (2) Divide the Western opponents of the Soviet Union by driving wedges between them and disrupting alliance systems. (3) Retain the primacy of the USSR in the Communist world. (4) Promote "proletarian internationalism," and those "national liberation movements" which are under Communist control or serve Soviet interests. (5) Minimize risks and avoid serious involvements on more than one front at any given time. This study, building on these earlier works, will demonstrate how the Soviets use specific political instrumentalities to achieve these objectives.

Strategy and the Correlation of Forces

In pursuit of their foreign policy objectives, the Soviets during the post-World War II period have developed a complex political-military strategy.[12] However, Moscow's deployment of diverse elements of this strategy at any given time is determined on the basis of its assessment of world power, termed the "correlation of forces." According to one specialist, "historically, the general concept . . . has been used since pre-revolutionary days to denote the relative alignment of two opposing forces or groups of forces . . . in the domestic arena, on the international scene, and to particular types of forces (for example, the correlation of class forces, of political forces, of economic forces, and of military forces)."[13]

The Soviet view of the correlation of forces often is misunderstood in the West. Many Western observers inappropriately have compared the concept with the "balance of power."[14] In addition to military factors, as Vernon Aspaturian has pointed out, "the 'correlation of forces' derives from a myriad of cross-cutting and interacting variables." Further, he notes, "the West is not as versed as the Soviet side in manipulating or adjusting to the manifold social, political, and revolutionary processes which contribute to the 'correlation of forces' equation."[15] In other words, while the notion of "balance of power" in Western usage tends to concentrate on the military and economic elements of power, the "correlation of forces" concept reflects the much broader understanding of power held by leaders in the Soviet Union.[16]

What are these "cross-cutting and interacting variables" noted by Aspaturian? How do they fit into Soviet political-military strategy? A brief review of Soviet sources reveals that this power equation is based on major categories or elements of power—military forces, economic forces, political forces, and international movements—which reflect the tensions and contradictions in the adversary's camp.[17] A great deal of Western confusion concerning the "correlation of forces" can be attributed to uncertainty regarding political forces, international movements, and contradictions in the non-Communist world, which are difficult to measure. However, according to Soviet commentary, these components of national and international politics play a very important role in framing foreign policy:[18]

> The foreign policy potential of a state is dependent not only upon its own forces and internal resources but, to a considerable extent, on such external factors as the existence of *reliable socio-political allies* among other states, a *national contingent of congenial classes*, *mass international movements*, and *other forces* active on the world scene. [Emphasis added.]

Influencing these national and international political and social forces appears to constitute an important objective in Soviet strategy. In the Soviet view, such efforts—if effectively directed—can play an important role in shifting the overall correlation of forces in favor of the USSR.[19]

In sum, Moscow's determination regarding which military and non-military elements of its strategy should be employed at a particular point in time is based on an assessment of the correlation of forces. This assessment is utilized to set offensive and defensive priorities, allocate resources, and determine actions to be undertaken. From the Soviet perspective, the nation that is able to gain the advantage in the correlation of forces will find itself in a preferable position to achieve its objectives. Shifts in the power equation result from both military and non-military factors. The importance of political and social elements in the correlation of forces is evident in the relevant Soviet sources.[20]

An examination of the years between 1960 and 1980 demonstrates that the leadership of the CPSU regards active measures as an indispensable component of Soviet strategy. Moscow employed these measures in various ways throughout this period. Both overt propaganda and covert political techniques were utilized extensively in the early 1960s, for example, when the Soviet Union was in an inferior military position vis-à-vis the United States and NATO. This is not surprising. Since the time of Lenin, the Soviets have relied on political warfare measures to attack and weaken their stronger opponents. Likewise, these measures continued to play a central role during the late 1970s and the early 1980s, when the Soviets made the claim that the correlation of forces had shifted in their favor.[21]

As will be demonstrated later, detente in the 1970s does not appear to have lowered the intensity or ameliorated the harsh nature of the Soviet propaganda directed at the United States and NATO. According to Brezhnev himself, detente did signal a lessening of US-Soviet tensions—as a result of both America's rapidly declining political and military commitments and its recognition of the growing power of Soviet military forces. Brezhnev also stressed, however, that detente did not reduce the international competition between "different social systems, with differing ideologies . . . stemming from these class differences." According to the Soviet leader, the easing of tension by no means calls off the struggle of ideas. This struggle is an objective phenomenon.[22]

Soviet Active Measures

Political warfare—the threat to employ or the actual use of overt and covert political, economic, and military techniques to influence politics and events in foreign countries—has been an instrument of policy since ancient times. Discussions of the subject can be found in the oldest manuals on political-military strategy and statecraft. For instance, Sun Tzu's *The Art of War*, written in China in the fifth century BC, stresses the importance of undermining the enemy's will through the use of agents who can "create cleavages between the sovereign and his ministers" and "leak information which is actually false."[23] The ancient Indian political classic, Kautilya's *Arthasastra*, likewise contains detailed advice on how to destroy the morale of political adversaries, both through spreading rumors and engaging in political intrigue.[24] Similar instruction in the methods of statecraft was set forth during the period of the Persian empires (the third through seventh centuries AD).[25]

During the twentieth century, various techniques of political warfare have been employed by many governments. However, some regimes have utilized these tactics in a much more systematic, dynamic, and integrated fashion than have others. Certainly Nazi Germany and Soviet Russia stand out as modern-day pioneers in both the theory and the practice of political warfare.[26]

During the 1950s and the 1960s, American views toward and utilization of overt and covert political warfare measures in many ways were marked by conceptual confusion and a degree of organizational compartmentalization. (By the 1970s, dissatisfaction with covert action had become so widespread that the United States apparently decided to greatly deemphasize the use of this policy instrument.[27]) To begin with, there was considerable disagreement over what constituted political warfare. For many years, students of the subject utilized the concept interchangeably with psychological warfare, ideological warfare, propaganda warfare, economic warfare, international propaganda, and the war of ideas.[28] Each of these terms has been variously used, according to the outlook of each individual writer, to identify a broad or narrow range of techniques.[29]

Among the major American political scientists, Harold Lasswell defined political warfare in the most inclusive terms:[30]

The idea of psychological warfare is somewhat less comprehensive. . . . The more inclusive conception is that of political warfare, which covers the use of more than the means of mass communication. Political warfare adds the important idea that all instruments of policy need to be properly correlated. . . . Diplomacy, for example, can be used to keep potential enemies neutral or to detach allies from the enemy. . . . When we speak of diplomacy, we have in mind the making of official comments. Whereas mass communications aims to large audiences, diplomacy proceeds by means of official negotiations. . . . Political warfare also includes the use of economic means.

Lasswell thus included diplomacy, propaganda, and economic warfare in his conceptualization of political warfare. His definition was not all-inclusive, however, for some relevant concepts were excluded. In effect, Lasswell separated the overt from the covert.[31]

When viewed in historical perspective, the approach of the United States government to covert foreign policy activities is relatively unusual. Many states regard the overt and covert influencing of politics abroad as part of the normal functioning of the entire foreign policy bureaucracy. They do not treat these categories of measures separately, and do not develop special terms to distinguish between them. In the early 1950s, however, the American government bureaucratically compartmentalized political warfare. Responsibility for covert activities was assigned to a special bureaucracy—the Central Intelligence Agency (CIA).

The United States also developed a specific term, "covert action," for these measures. It is true that various interagency mechanisms were established to coordinate the functions of the different bureaucratic elements involved in political warfare. Nevertheless, a sharp distinction between overt and covert behavior was reflected in both organization and policy.[32] According to one student of the subject, "Americans have continued to look upon secret means of bringing influence to bear as somehow beyond the pale of ordinary foreign policy. The very terms 'covert action' and 'special activities' have tended to signify that . . . they are made of different stuff than is the substance of foreign policy."[33] In the Soviet view, however, no such distinctions are apparent.

The Soviets now use the term "active measures" to describe overt and covert techniques for influencing events and behavior in, and the actions of, foreign societies. There is no exact equivalent in the Western lexicon. While there are similarities between Soviet active measures and some Western activities, important differences also exist. First, while Moscow has long-term global ambitions, the objectives of Western political influence techniques are much more restricted. Second, the means utilized in Soviet active measures are virtually unlimited. Soviet practitioners apparently are constrained primarily by prudence and the requirements of efficiency. By contrast, Western leaders usually also are constrained by major cultural, political, and moral considerations.

Additionally, the Politburo has the organizational capability to orchestrate and centralize overt and covert means to achieve its objectives. Western nations, particularly the United States, are far too pluralistic to achieve a great deal of central coordination, except in the most unusual circumstances. Soviet leaders also engage in active measures campaigns for lengthy periods of time. Western governments, on the other hand, change frequently and are subject to shifts in public opinion. These are among the major differences between the Soviet capability to conduct active measures and Western instrumentalities. Indeed, of twentieth century regimes, only Nazi Germany has rivaled Moscow and its allies in the appreciation, understanding, and utilization of these foreign policy tools.[34]

A review of the origins and development of the political system of the USSR bears out the importance of these techniques to Soviet leaders.[35] Such an examination demonstrates as well that Moscow's recent and current use of active measures is undergirded by long experience and practice. It is well documented that the Bolshevik seizure of power relied largely on a combination of propaganda and political influence techniques, as well as armed force, to bring down the provisional government.[36] In effect, current Soviet techniques represent a logical outgrowth of the Bolshevik struggle for power, especially during the period between the two revolutions of 1917.

However, in some ways current methods also reflect the traditions of the messianic Russian revolutionary movement. From its beginning, it relied on the creation of broad fronts, the enlistment of agents, and other techniques of political warfare. Given this background, it is not surprising that after the Bolshevik revolution first Lenin and then Stalin applied these measures not only against the remnants of non-Communist forces in the new Soviet state, but also against rival factions in the CPSU. The campaigns against Trotsky—who was dubbed first a "Menshevik," then an enemy of the Soviet state, and finally an outright Nazi German and Japanese agent—serve as good examples.

In its conduct of foreign activities over the decades, the Soviet state simply has institutionalized and refined these practices. Leonard Schapiro, reflecting on over sixty years of Soviet foreign policy, has noted that once the Bolsheviks had come to power, these tactics became central instruments for the achievement of Soviet international objectives. According to Schapiro:[37]

> The use of an overwhelming military presence and the maximum espionage and subversion presence are part of what has always been described in Soviet terminology as "ideological struggle," which is repeatedly asserted as the necessary concomitant of "peaceful coexistence." . . . In essence, this view is the logical implementation of Lenin's policy of combining trade and correct diplomatic relations, on the one hand, with subversion and political warfare, on the other.

For the Soviet Union, active measures constitute a dynamic and integrated array of overt and covert techniques for influencing events and behavior in, and the actions of, foreign countries. These measures are employed to influence the policies of other governments, undermine confidence in the leaders and institutions of these states, disrupt the relations between various nations, and discredit and weaken major opponents.[38] This frequently involves attempts to deceive the target and to distort the target's perceptions of reality.

Active measures may be carried out overtly through officially-sponsored propaganda channels, the conduct of diplomatic relations, and involvement in international cultural affairs activities. Soviet means for conducting active measures covertly include a broad range of political techniques. Covert propaganda is employed in an ongoing effort to influence the media in foreign countries, and hence to influence local audiences. In this connection, Moscow endeavors to place Soviet-authored or -inspired articles in foreign publications, either minus any indication of source or with attribution to a non-Soviet author.[39] A second technique, which in the last few years has received increasing public attention in the West, is disinformation. The objective of disinformation (described in detail below) is to manipulate target persons and groups to believe in the veracity of the message and consequently to act in the interests of the nation conducting the operation. Other covert techniques employed by the Soviet Union include the use of international front organizations, the sponsorship of clandestine radio broadcasts, and the carrying out of agent-of-influence operations.

Also included as a component of Soviet active measures are military maneuvers and paramilitary operations. This can involve various forms of deception, as well as secret support to insurgency movements and terrorist groups. Special personnel and organizational means have been established for these activities. Specialized training for terrorist and insurgent movements is offered in the USSR, Eastern Europe, Cuba, and the Middle East; arms and other forms of military assistance are provided; and Soviet or proxy advisors may be deployed to an area of conflict. The Soviet military establishment, as well as the Committee for State Security (KGB), plays a significant organizational role in the conduct of political and military deception and paramilitary operations. The General Staff oversees military aid, while the Chief Intelligence Directorate of the Soviet General Staff (GRU) plays a role through both its intelligence training and its insurgency branch.

This study, however, will concentrate only on media activities and political influence operations.

SOVIET ORGANIZATIONAL STRUCTURE FOR ACTIVE MEASURES

Organizational Structure

Most Western specialists on the USSR believe that Soviet decisions regarding major policy matters are made at the apex of the CPSU structure. Schapiro, Frederick Barghoorn, Robert Conquest, Merle Fainsod, John Reshetar, and John Armstrong (among others) have described the Soviet decision-making structure and process along the lines set forth in the following paragraphs.[40] Although mentioned only briefly in the Soviet constitution, it is the CPSU which determines the basic policies of the regime, which then are adopted and carried out by the Soviet government.

At the apex of the party structure is the Politburo, the ruling body of the Soviet system. Apart from its membership and the fact that it constitutes the site of origin for all major decisions, little is known about this highest Soviet policy-making body. According to Reshetar, "Central Committee resolutions usually reflect Politburo decisions and the Politburo also issues directives to various government ministries and agencies. It takes up urgent problems brought before it by the departments of the Party Secretariat, by a ministry, or by the Council of Ministers."[41]

This is not meant to imply that Soviet centralized decision-making always operates unencumbered by conflict. As Armstrong has observed, "the Soviet political system has been frequently racked by severe conflicts." Armstrong goes on to note, however, that "what Communist ideology, as an element of political culture, accomplished was to keep the resolution of these conflicts largely within the institutional framework of the Communist Party."[42] In other words, whether or not a major policy decision causes friction within the centralized Party structure, the decision process remains the domain of the Politburo (or a small circle within it, such as the Defense Council).

How important a role does the Politburo play in decisions related to active measures? The available literature on Soviet policy-making and the contentious nature of many of these techniques both suggest that the Politburo is heavily involved. It approves the general policies and themes which guide major political warfare campaigns, and reviews their outcome and effectiveness. These political tactics have remained of considerable importance to the Soviet leadership since the early days of CPSU rule. Hence, it seems logical that the Politburo would retain oversight with respect to all major decisions concerning these policies and programs. All known sources indicate that this likely is the case, but little confirmed information actually demonstrating this fact is available.

While we are not privy to the internal planning process of the Politburo, an examination of key factors related to the Soviet organizational structure for conducting active measures does provide identifiable indicators of the importance the top leadership places in these activities. These indicators include the positions within the top CPSU organizational command structure held by the three key bodies with responsibility for planning, coordinating, and conducting active measures; the historical roots of these departments, and their growth during the period under examination; the importance of the Party leaders who direct these departments; and the relationship between broad Soviet foreign policy goals and the policies and themes of

Moscow's major overt propaganda and covert political programs.

Chart I identifies the three major organs—the International Department (ID), the International Information Department (IID), and the KGB—responsible for planning and conducting specific programs in support of the major active measures campaigns established by the Politburo. As indicated by the direction of the arrows, authority for the planning, directing, and coordinating of programs is centralized within these three CPSU operational departments. This centralization of control reflects Soviet views regarding the existence and value of an organizational weapon. Starting with the revolutionary period, Lenin emphasized that no separation exists between words, actions, and organization.[43] Wilbur Schramm, reflecting on the evolution and the interrelationship of these elements of active measures, explains that:[44]

> the word does not typically stand alone in Soviet planning. From the very first, Communists were told by their leaders that words were not enough, that words had to merge with deeds, and both into organization.... When we try to describe Soviet psychological operations, therefore, we talk not so much about a word weapon as about an organization weapon.

It is beyond the scope of this study to review the growth and development since 1917 of Soviet active measures. It should be noted, however, that this component of Soviet foreign policy behavior has passed through several specific phases. Until roughly 1930, active measures in large part were the domain of the Comintern. The intelligence and security service (the Cheka and its successors) appears to have focused its attention on suppressing counterrevolutionary forces within the USSR and dealing with Russian emigres abroad. (In the case of the emigres, these efforts did involve the intelligence service in active measures campaigns abroad.) Under Stalin's domination, active measures were synchronized, with all Soviet agencies

CHART I

Soviet Organizational Structure for Active Measures

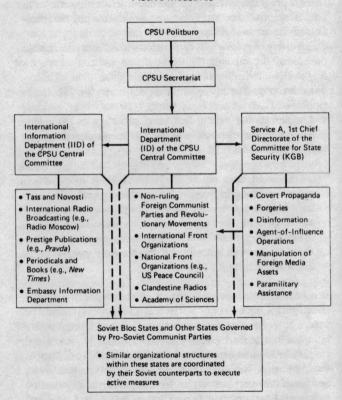

CPSU Politburo

CPSU Secretariat

International Information Department (IID) of the CPSU Central Committee

International Department (ID) of the CPSU Central Committee

Service A, 1st Chief Directorate of the Committee for State Security (KGB)

- Tass and Novosti
- International Radio Broadcasting (e.g., Radio Moscow)
- Prestige Publications (e.g., *Pravda*)
- Periodicals and Books (e.g., *New Times*)
- Embassy Information Department

- Non-ruling Foreign Communist Parties and Revolutionary Movements
- International Front Organizations
- National Front Organizations (e.g., US Peace Council)
- Clandestine Radios
- Academy of Sciences

- Covert Propaganda
- Forgeries
- Disinformation
- Agent-of-Influence Operations
- Manipulation of Foreign Media Assets
- Paramilitary Assistance

Soviet Bloc States and Other States Governed by Pro-Soviet Communist Parties

- Similar organizational structures within these states are coordinated by their Soviet counterparts to execute active measures

involved in foreign affairs now expected to participate in these efforts. The purges of the Stalinist era, however, served to hamper the effectiveness of these activities. The post-1945 era, characterized by Moscow's newly heightened position in world affairs, has seen a proliferation and further refinement of propaganda and political influence techniques, as well as the further development of organizational mechanisms for planning, coordinating, and conducting these measures.

A closer look at the ID, the IID, and the KGB now is in order.

The International Department

An important feature of Soviet foreign policy is the network of close links the CPSU has maintained with almost all Communist parties, both ruling and non-ruling, around the world. In the period between World War I and World War II, the CPSU maintained relations with other Communist parties and with international front organizations largely through the Third International, or Comintern.[45] Stalin disbanded the Comintern in 1943 (supposedly as a gesture of good will to the Allies); and during the post-World War II period, the responsibilities of the Comintern were reassigned to certain key departments of the CPSU Central Committee.

While it is not clear precisely when these departments were created, Schapiro has established the following:[46]

It was only after the Comintern had been dissolved (1943) that the Central Committee acquired a foreign affairs department which it had hitherto lacked. . . . Thus, the Foreign Affairs Department became for practical purposes the successor to the Comintern. But it was much more. For some time the new Foreign Affairs Department functioned as a complex of a variety of activities in the foreign field.

According to Schapiro, in 1957 the Foreign Affairs Department was divided into three separate and independent Central Committee departments: "a Department for Relations with Communist and Workers Parties of Socialist Countries, which controls the bloc; a Department for Cadres Abroad, closely linked to the KGB, which is responsible for the instruction of foreign cells of the CPSU, that is to say cells inside the foreign missions"; and the International Department.[47]

It is important to view these developments within the broader context of Soviet foreign policy. First, they build clearly on the tradition of the Comintern, established by Lenin as one of several tools for conducting the political warfare element of Soviet foreign policy. Second, the separation and specification of roles described above marked a critical juncture in the post-World War II expansion of Soviet capabilities for political warfare. Finally, it should be noted that the personalities associated with two of these new departments during the 1960–1980 period eventually rose to prominence in the Soviet leadership.

With respect to this latter factor, the career of Boris Ponomarev, *de facto* head of the ID, is discussed below. The first head of the CPSU Department for relations with ruling Communist parties was Yuri Andropov (who probably was appointed in 1957). Immediately prior to this appointment, Andropov apparently worked for the Ministry of Foreign Affairs, where his posts included those of Counsellor, and later Ambassador to Budapest (during the 1956 Hungarian revolution). Andropov was not a Ministry of Foreign Affairs career diplomat; rather, he probably was connected with the Foreign Affairs Department of the Central Committee (which had inherited the mantle of the Comintern), specializing in political warfare.[48] In 1967 he became the head of the KGB.

Of the three Central Committee departments created in 1957, the International Department appears to be the most important. The true significance of the ID—headed by Ponomarev since its inception—often is overlooked in the West. According to one recent study, "mistakenly, the International Department is believed by some Western authorities to deal solely with relations with non-ruling Communist Parties. . . . But even a cursory glance at this department shows that it enjoys much greater prestige than other departments."[49]

In the view of Schapiro, the ID is even more important than the Soviet Ministry of Foreign Affairs. Schapiro has written: "it seems therefore beyond dispute that the International Department is the element in the Soviet decisionmaking process which gathers information on foreign policy, briefs the Politburo, and thereby exercises, subject to the Politburo, decisive influence on Soviet foreign policy."[50] This view also is supported by former KGB officer Stanislav Levchenko, who specialized in active measures operations. (Levchenko defected in 1979, and is interviewed extensively in Chapter V of this study.)

Chart I graphically outlines the activities of the International Department in foreign policy, identifying its various functions. With respect to the point made by Schapiro, we see that the ID coordinates and reviews inputs concerning Soviet foreign policy matters from the Ministry of Foreign Affairs, the KGB, and various "think tanks" under the Academy of Sciences.[51] Some experts believe that in addition to coordinating and reviewing such information, representatives of the ID in foreign embassies assess political trends, and establish contacts with "progressive" organizations and individuals in these states.[52]

The role of the ID in political warfare is conducted through its liaison with similar departments in Soviet bloc countries, and through its relationship with non-ruling Communist parties and revolutionary movements. In addition to ID involvement in international meetings, ID representatives with responsibility for persuading these parties and movements to carry out overt and covert propaganda and political action campaigns on behalf of the USSR are posted both temporarily and permanently within Soviet embassies abroad.[53] In conjunction with these efforts, the ID is responsible for the publication of the monthly journal *Problems of Peace and Socialism*, known in its English-language edition as *World Marxist Review*. Through the *Review*, an official source of Soviet ideology for foreign audiences, the ID openly communicates instruction to foreign Communist parties, revolutionary movements, and front organizations.

The ID also has responsibility for administering, funding, and coordinating well over a dozen major, ostensibly non-governmental, international front organizations established since World War II. The fronts are yet another means through which the ID conducts active measures. The major international fronts include:[54]

1. World Peace Council (WPC)	Established in 1949. Principal activities focus on Soviet peace campaigns, publications, congresses, and coordination of other international fronts.
2. World Federation of Trade Unions (WFTU)	Established in 1945. Principal focus is coordination of Communist trade unions worldwide, publications, training, financing, educational programs, and seeking "unity" between Communist and non-Communist unions.
3. Afro-Asian People's Solidarity Organization (AAPSO)	Established in 1957. Principal function is to serve as a channel for Soviet influence in the Third World.
4. World Federation of Democratic Youth (WFDY)	Established in 1945. Principal function is to support Soviet peace campaigns through publications, congresses, and World Youth Festivals.
5. International Union of Students (IUS)	Established in 1946. Principal functions are quite similar to those of the WFDY.

6. International Institute for Peace (IIP)

Established in 1958. Closely associated with the WPC. Principal function is to direct the Forum for East-West Discussions Between Scientists.

7. International Organization of Journalists (IOJ)

Established in 1952. Principal function is to support Soviet peace campaigns, human rights campaigns, and other causes through publications, conferences, and similar activities.

8. Christian Peace Conference (CPC)

Established in 1958. Principal function is to develop Christian and theological support for Soviet peace policies.

9. Women's International Democratic Federation (WIDF)

Established in 1945. Principal activities focus on publications, meetings, and seminars in support of general Soviet foreign policy goals.

10. International Association of Democratic Lawyers (IADL)

Established in 1946. Principal activities are publications and conferences in support of general Soviet foreign policy goals.

In a later chapter we will examine in detail the role of the leading front group, the World Peace Council, with a focus on the WPC propaganda campaign directed against the United States and NATO during the 1960–1980 period.

Finally, the ID has been responsible for operating a number of clandestine radios. One of the best known of these is the National Voice of Iran, which has been operating out of Baku since 1959.[55]

The status of ID head Ponomarev serves as a further indication of the importance of this department within the CPSU. Prior to assuming the directorship of the ID, Ponomarev was an important official in the Comintern.[56] The key positions he now holds are Secretary of the Central Committee, candidate member of the Politburo, and Chairman of the Foreign Affairs Commission of one of the chambers of the Supreme Soviet. Additionally, Ponomarev's writing over the years has established him as a leading official voice concerning theoretical issues related to Soviet doctrine on international relations, especially with respect to proletarian internationalism and the Soviet role in assisting its growth and expansion.[57]

The International Information Department

The dissemination abroad of Soviet overt propaganda is accomplished by Party, governmental, and social organizations, all operating under Party supervision. Prior to 1978, these activities were under the control of the Department of Agitation and Propaganda (Agitprop) of the CPSU Central Committee. According to Barghoorn, this department had dual responsibility for the coordination of both domestic and foreign propaganda.[58] In other words, the Party ensured its control of all organizations engaged in foreign propaganda activities by the same methods of centralized CPSU control that were employed throughout the Soviet state.

The Department of Agitation and Propaganda provided policy guidance and control of those operational committees within the Council of Ministers of the USSR which were engaged in foreign information and propaganda activities (e.g., the Committee on the Press, the Committee on Radio Broadcasting and Television, the Committee on Cinematography, etc.).[59] In 1947, Mikhail Suslov was appointed Head of the Department of Agitation and Propaganda and Secretary of the Central Committee. Although Suslov joined the Presidium in 1952, and under Brezhnev rose to considerable power and influence in the Politburo, "supervision of propaganda campaigns, enforcement of ideological campaigns, control of Soviet journalism and culture, and relations with foreign Communist Parties" remained his special domain.[60]

It appears that in 1965, the post-Khrushchev leadership sought to improve the quality of Soviet propaganda through the creation of a new department of the Central Committee. Identified as the Information Department, this body was headed by Dmitrii Shevlyagin (who had served as Deputy Head of the International Department since its creation in 1957).[61] Little is known about the composition and functions of this department; and by the late 1960s, it may have been discarded as an unsuccessful experiment. All references to the Information Department stopped at this time. Its director was appointed Soviet Ambassador to Algeria in 1968, and a successor to head the Information Department was never announced.

In 1978, in a move apparently designed to improve the coordination of what was already an impressive program of foreign propaganda activities, the CPSU established the International Information Department (IID) of the Central Committee.[62] Not a great deal is known about the IID. Some Western analysts believe it was created to improve Soviet foreign propaganda through more centralized and efficient integration of the wide range of vehicles employed.

It is difficult to ascertain, however, the actual importance of this department. Chart I identifies the various propaganda channels whose output the IID appears to have responsibility for integrating. Available evidence, however, tends to support the contention of former KGB officer Levchenko that the IID neither sets the propaganda line for these communication channels nor has responsibility for their programmatic guidance. According to a June 14, 1981 speech by Politburo member K. U. Chernenko to the CPSU Central Committee, the International Department has responsibility for these functions.[63] Levchenko also states that the IID carries much less significance than the ID. He asserts that it is the ID, and not the IID, that sets the overt propaganda line (under Politburo direction). Furthermore, he explains, the IID is not the equal of the ID in terms of numbers of personnel and other organizational indicators.

Whatever the limitations of the IID, the fact that this body was created serves as yet another indicator of the desire of the Soviet leadership to ensure effective use of active measures programs. Further evidence can be seen in the selection of Leonard Zamyatin to head the IID. Zamyatin, a member of the Central Committee, became Head of the Press Department of the Ministry of Foreign Affairs in 1962, and was promoted in 1970 to serve as director of the Soviet news agency, TASS. In each of these prior positions, Zamyatin directed important components of the USSR's foreign propaganda machine; and in the case of TASS, he supervised its growth and development.

The formation of the IID was only the most recent step in a series of measures undertaken to improve the Soviet foreign propaganda program. A brief examination of the growth and development over the past two decades of a wide variety of Soviet foreign propaganda outlets[64] provides additional evidence concerning the important role the top Soviet leadership assigns to propaganda. Now coordinated by the IID (see Chart I), these outlets include the foreign radio broadcasting system, two news agencies, the prestige press, various publications, and approximately 500 Soviet journalists stationed in foreign countries.

Foreign radio broadcasting clearly has played a central role in the Soviet international propaganda effort. External broadcasting greatly expanded during the 1960–1980 period: in 1960, weekly hours of international broadcasting (with some duplication of programming) totaled approximately 1047; by 1970 this figure had more than doubled, to 2,155; and by 1980 the total hours broadcast per week had reached 2,762.[65] (See Chart II.)

In addition to Radio Moscow, the Soviets broadcast through various regional radio stations, including Radio Erevan, Kiev Radio, Radio Tashkent, and Radio Peace and Progress (RPP), which broadcasts from the USSR to the Third World. These regional stations, as one might expect, play a special role in Soviet foreign propaganda operations. For example, RPP—purported to be the voice of Soviet "public opinion"—is directed primarily at mass audiences in the Third World.[66] Since it is supposed to have no connection with the official government, RPP tends to be more outspoken and less sophisticated than, say, Radio Moscow.

External broadcasts are conducted in over 80 languages and dialects, including Radio Moscow's "World Service" in English (broadcasting on all short-wave bands 24 hours per day). By comparison, in 1981 weekly hours of American international broadcasting stood at 905 for the Voice of America, 553 for Radio Free Europe, and 469 for Radio Liberty—a total of 1,927 hours weekly, in 46 languages.[67]

Similar growth in other foreign propaganda outlets also occurred during the 1960–1980 period. For example, an unofficial news agency—Novosti Press Agency (APN)—was created in the early 1960s to assist TASS, the authoritative official government voice. During the late 1960s and the early 1970s, TASS maintained bureaus and correspondents in almost 100 countries, and 62 foreign agencies, national information services, and radio and television companies in 60 countries directly received and used its services. By the late 1970s, these latter figures had grown to 300 foreign agencies, services, and companies in 93 countries.[68]

Like Radio Peace and Progress, Novosti supposedly represents the voice of Soviet public opinion (including such information and cultural organizations as the Union of Journalists, the Union of Writers, and the Union of Soviet Societies of Friendship and Cultural Ties with Foreign Countries). In reality, its activities are coordinated by the Kremlin. By the early 1970s, Novosti (APN) had developed an impressive array of assets:[69]

> APN exchanges information with 101 international and national agencies, 120 publishing firms, more than 100 radio and television companies, and more than 7,000 of the world's largest newspapers and magazines. It maintains bureaus and correspondents in 80 countries. APN claims an annual transmission to foreign media of 60,000 literary pieces and more than 2 million photographic prints.

CHART II

Weekly Hours* of Soviet Foreign Broadcasting

	1960	1962	1964	1966	1968	1970	1972	1974	1976	1978	1980
Africa	42:00	112:00	129:30	147:00	164:30	169:00	169:00	169:00	169:00	274:00	270:30
East Asia & the Pacific	119:00	180:00	232:45	259:35	399:35	424:05	427:35	449:35	464:35	498:35	544:05
Europe	344:00	324:00	278:50	344:30	547:05	581:20	545:25	518:35	541:55	607:25	623:05
Latin America	56:00	120:00	95:30	132:40	137:00	139:30	139:30	138:30	131:00	152:30	133:00
Near East & North Africa	184:20	209:25	206:30	225:00	237:35	253:15	250:20	280:15	279:15	340:45	364:55
South Asia	80:30	71:45	12:00	136:30	202:00	247:30	247:30	211:00	219:00	309:00	370:15
North America	158:00	105:30	88:00	111:10	111:30	111:30	108:00	107:00	128:30	205:30	222:15
Radio Moscow "World Service"	63:05	81:10	195:15	210:20	228:20	229:15	229:30	266:10	269:30	226:30	234:30
TOTAL	1046:55	1203:50	1238:20	1566:45	2027:35	2155:25	2116:50	2140:05	2202:45	2614:15	2762:35

*With some duplication of programming.

Sources: *External Information and Cultural Relations Programs of the Union of Soviet Socialist Republics* (Washington, DC: USIA Office of Research and Assessment, 1973); *Soviet External Radio Broadcasts, 1970-1978* (Washington, DC: USIA Office of Research, 1979); and *Communist International Radio Broadcasting in 1980* (Washington, DC: USIA Office of Research).

Under various intergovernmental agreements, APN also provides the material for 52 Soviet magazines, 8 newspapers, and 119 press bulletins which are published abroad. These have a combined unit circulation of 2.7 million copies.

Moscow also employs the prestige press (most importantly, *Pravda*) and a wide range of publications for foreign propaganda purposes. According to one source:[70]

> in the mid-seventies the USSR . . . published 91 journals and magazines in 20 foreign languages for circulation abroad. . . . This total is far surpassed by the additional number and circulation of periodicals printed abroad and available either commercially or through embassies and friendship societies. Some 100 million copies were estimated to reach local populations through these channels.

While not all of these publications are designed to serve foreign policy objectives, journals such as *New Times*, *International Affairs*, and *World Marxist Review* are specifically directed toward this end. Prestigious publications such as *Pravda* (which has a worldwide circulation) frequently are used to initiate new propaganda themes or float new stories related to old themes, which then are replayed and amplified by Radio Moscow, TASS, and other outlets of Soviet foreign propaganda.

In addition to the conduct of overt propaganda, TASS, Novosti, and vehicles of Soviet journalism in general are known to harbor a percentage (sometimes quite large) of KGB officers among their domestic and overseas personnel. In Chapter V, Levchenko maintains that *New Times* in the mid-1970s had twelve foreign correspondents, of which ten were KGB officers.

Another (and controversial) indicator of the growth and development of Soviet overt propaganda is the magnitude of the financial resources devoted to these efforts. Estimates of Soviet spending (in US dollars) are difficult to calculate,[71] but available information supports the contention that the Kremlin regards this area as important. In 1978, the head of Clandestine Operations at the CIA cited the following estimates of annual Soviet expenditures for key foreign propaganda outlets during the latter years of the 1970s: TASS, $550 million; Novosti, $500 million; *Pravda*, $250 million; *New Times*, $200 million; and Radio Moscow foreign service, $700 million. By comparison, it is estimated that Moscow's annual expenditures ($150 million per year) for jamming US broadcasts are greater than the costs of operating the Voice of America, Radio Free Europe, and Radio Liberty combined.[72] The CIA's rough estimate for overall Soviet spending in 1978 for propaganda and covert action was approximately $3 billion.[73] An estimate made in 1982 raised the approximate annual figure to $4 billion.[74]

The Committee for State Security (KGB)

As Chart I depicts, a third major instrument available to the CPSU leadership is the Committee for State Security, or KGB. The origins of the KGB can be traced to December 20, 1917, when the Council of People's Commissars established the All-Russian Extraordinary Commission for Combatting Counter-revolution and Sabotage (Cheka). Established primarily as an investigative body, the Cheka quickly transformed itself into an instrument of terror to eliminate opposition to Bolshevik rule both at home and abroad. With the end of the civil war and the consolidation of Communist power, it became expedient to make some cosmetic changes in the state security apparatus. A decree abolishing the Cheka and replacing it with the State Political Directorate (GPU) was issued on February 6, 1922.

Since the days of the Cheka, the state security apparatus has been reorganized and retitled many times, becoming successively the GPU, the OGPU, the GUGB/NKVD, the NKGB, the MGB, and—on March 13, 1954—the KGB. It is germane to note, however, that while the state security apparatus underwent significant organizational alterations and expansion over the years, there exists an institutional credo and spirit that ran directly from the Cheka to the KGB. In other words, a sense of tradition and continuity in the state security apparatus has endured and flourished since 1917. In fact, antecedents for virtually all operational departments of the KGB can be found in the Cheka. Furthermore, dedicated KGB officers boast of their Chekist heritage.[75]

As the "sword and shield" of the CPSU, the KGB has responsibility for internal security functions, for foreigners visiting or residing in the Soviet Union, and for counter-intelligence. It also has responsibility for all clandestine operations conducted abroad, except for those assigned to the Chief Intelligence Directorate of the Soviet General Staff (GRU). Finally, through its border guards, which number between 300,000 and 400,000 highly trained and indoctrinated troops, the KGB secures the long borders of the USSR.

The external operations of the KGB always have fallen into two interrelated and frequently overlapping categories: straight-forward espionage (including counterintelligence) and political warfare.[76] In the case of the latter, the KGB employs a diverse range of covert tactics designed to support and supplement overt measures.

The coordination between overt and covert active measures is not always apparent, as will be demonstrated by the following overview of KGB operations. Covert techniques utilized by the KGB include covert (i.e., falsely attributed) propaganda, agent-of-influence operations, and oral and written disinformation (including forgeries). While these measures have been separated here for purposes of analysis, in fact they often are interrelated in practice.

Covert propaganda frequently is used to reinforce themes promoted through Soviet outlets of overt propaganda. This tactic takes two general forms: the clandestine placement of a media item in a foreign news outlet, or the selective replay of an article which originally appeared in a foreign publication. In the former case, the Soviets seek to create credibility for an other-wise implausible argument by achieving foreign placement of the material through a non-Soviet journalist (who may be witting or unwitting of the Soviet connection). In the latter case, the content and meaning of a public statement by a prominent figure or a story from a well-known foreign newspaper are shaped to serve Soviet objectives, and then are replayed through both overt and covert channels.

A second technique employed by the KGB involves agent-of-influence operations. The purpose of such an operation is to covertly inject Soviet views into governmental, political, journalistic, business, labor, and academic circles of a foreign country. To accomplish this objective, KGB officers develop relationships with key figures from these influential circles who are willing to collaborate (wittingly or unwittingly) on matters of mutual interest. In return for this collaboration, the KGB will assist the agent of influence in his or her particular undertakings. In those cases in which the agent is a journalist, the connection with covert propaganda operations is apparent. (In a later chapter, a detailed account of one such operation will be presented.)

Since the early days of the regime, forgery—one of a number of disinformation activities—has been used by the Soviet intelligence services. Forgery entails using either a genuine document which has been altered, or the complete fabrication of a document. In a later chapter, this study examines two sets of forgeries from the early 1960s and the late 1970s which were used to discredit the United States and NATO.

Another category of active measures in which the KGB is involved is paramilitary operations, composed of a wide range of Soviet activities in support of terrorist groups and insurgency movements. Among the measures employed most frequently over the last decade are covert provision of arms and logistical support, specialized political and military training, and advisory support by the Soviet intelligence and security services.[77]

Within the KGB today, responsibility for directing most of the activities described above rests with Service A of the First Chief Directorate. However, as in the case of the International Department, Service A apparently is the result of a process of organizational evolution and expansion over the last two decades. There is reason to believe that the CPSU in the late 1950s undertook to escalate KGB use of disinformation and other forms of active measures against the United States and NATO.[78] To assist in this undertaking, a Disinformation Department (Department D) was established within the First Chief Directorate.[79] In addition to planning and supervising its own operations, Department D was to oversee similar activities conducted by the intelligence services of the Eastern bloc countries.[80]

In 1968, under the leadership of then-KGB chief Yuri Andropov, Department D was renamed Department A; and in the early 1970s, Andropov upgraded the Department to a Service—a change which presumably signified an increase in available resources and a higher position in the KGB organizational structure. Once again, these institutional developments serve as important indicators of the interest of the Soviet leadership in covert active measures.

OVERT PROPAGANDA AND COVERT POLITICAL TECHNIQUES: DISTINCTIONS AND DEFINITIONS

The remaining portion of this chapter identifies and describes in more detail the specific objectives and techniques selected for close examination in Chapters III and IV.

Overt Propaganda

Propaganda, in general, may be defined as written or oral information which deliberately seeks to influence and/or manipulate the opinions and attitudes of a given target grouping. A government may direct its propaganda toward either a domestic or a foreign mass audience. In the case of overt propaganda, no attempt is made to conceal the true source.

The origins of the important place held by propaganda in contemporary Soviet domestic and foreign policy can be found in the creation by Lenin in 1900 of *Iskra* ("Spark")—a newspaper that, according to Lenin, would "blow every spark of class struggle and popular indignation into a general conflagration."[81] This development established a permanent position for propaganda as a principal weapon in first the Bolshevik and then the CPSU arsenal. As Barghoorn has observed:[82]

> Lenin established a tradition within which Bolshevik "professional revolutionaries" and, later, specially trained functionaries of the Soviet state and of foreign Communist parties, have systematically employed modern communications techniques. . . .
>
> Obviously, the present leadership of the Soviet Union shares Lenin's concerns regarding the significance of propaganda as a political instrument.

Although Barghoorn's book appeared in the early 1960s, what he observed at that time continued to hold true throughout the twenty-year period between 1960 and 1980. Foreign propaganda remains a primary instrument of Soviet foreign policy.[83]

Since the early days of the post–World War II period, Western political systems have comprised the main target of Soviet propaganda. It appears that Moscow in the late 1950s initiated a new program designed to accelerate the quality, quantity, and intensity of this propaganda offensive. In his examination of two communiqués issued by the Soviets to ruling and non-ruling Communist parties in 1957 and 1960, Barghoorn has observed:[84]

> With the internal situation in the Soviet bloc once again under tight control late in 1957, apparently Moscow felt that the time was ripe for the resumption of the international propaganda and psychological warfare offensive. . . . Both communiques depicted the capitalist countries as fighting to preserve a deteriorating position of world power. The 1960 communique . . . referred to the contemporary historical period as a time of Socialist

revolutions . . . a time of the breakdown of imperialism. . . .

In keeping with this strategic analysis, the two communiques contained directives for propaganda tactics.

While the early stages of this campaign apparently were interrupted by the internal power struggle against Khrushchev, by the latter half of the 1960s the Soviet propaganda offensive again had begun to expand. In the latter half of the 1970s, the campaign against the United States and NATO was intensified further. It still continues today. Soviet foreign propaganda has been characterized by intensity and concentration; flexibility and adaptability; deception and manipulation; and centralized control and coordination.

With respect to the first characteristic, Moscow has demonstrated an ability to employ mass communications techniques to initiate major propaganda campaigns that can concentrate on a particular target for an extended period of time. For example, during the entire twenty-year period examined herein, a consistent theme of Soviet propaganda has been the unwillingness of the United States and NATO to ensure peace by disarming. The ultimate message—i.e., the militarism and imperialism of the United States and NATO stand in the way of the various disarmament plans proposed by the USSR—is repeated virtually *ad infinitum*. Further, when the international political situation related to a particular propaganda theme reaches a critical juncture, the intensity of the propaganda campaign is escalated rapidly. This was apparent, for example, during the latter half of the 1970s, when opposition in Western Europe to deployment of the neutron weapon and to the modernization of NATO's intermediate-range nuclear forces (INF) received increasingly frequent attention in Soviet propaganda.

Flexibility and adaptability are additional features of Soviet propaganda. The Soviets are able to rapidly adjust their efforts to changing issues and conditions, promptly coordinating words with actions. As will be demonstrated in the next chapter, this capability was especially salient during the latter half of the

1970s. That Soviet propaganda also utilizes intentional misrepresentation and exaggeration is not surprising, in view of the emphasis placed on the role of deception in the Soviet approach to political and military questions.[85] Finally, as explained earlier in this chapter, all Soviet propaganda activities are centrally controlled and coordinated at the apex of the Party structure.

It is important to note that Moscow also employs other techniques of overt propaganda, although a detailed examination of these measures is beyond the scope of this study. One important channel of communication, for example, is achieved through personal face-to-face contacts, and Moscow over the years has employed cultural exchange programs and friendship societies (in conjunction with other measures) as additional propaganda vehicles. These techniques have been examined in studies by Barghoorn, Sylvia Margulies, and Paul Hollander.[86]

Covert Political Techniques

While every state seeks to influence foreign governments and public opinion, the Soviets also use covert (i.e., secret) political techniques to increase dramatically the effectiveness of their overt propaganda and overt political efforts. These covert political techniques usually serve to reinforce, and are integrated with, Moscow's themes of overt propaganda. As with overt propaganda, covert techniques are massive in number and of long-term duration.

Because Moscow goes to enormous lengths to hide these activities, they are difficult to identify and categorize in their entirety. Nevertheless, it is possible to demonstrate and to document the Soviet employment during the 1960–1980 period of several forms of secret active measures—disinformation (often carried out through forgeries), the use of agents of influence in the media, and the promotion of covert propaganda by international front organizations—to amplify and augment overt propaganda directed against the United States and NATO. Much confusion and disagreement exists among specialists regarding the definition of these secret techniques and what each tactic entails. It is true that these categories are not easily distinguishable or separated, and the techniques often are interrelated in practice. Nevertheless, in the following pages we shall attempt to define each technique and to differentiate among them.

Until the 1950s, the term *dezinformatsia* was used in some Soviet circles to refer to what Soviet leaders now call "active measures." *Dezinformatsia* currently is used in Moscow to refer to a specific type of active measures technique, here called "disinformation." Of the covert political techniques emphasized here, only disinformation in recent years has received considerable public attention in the West. The subject, however, often has been misunderstood. What, then, is disinformation? In 1965, the CIA maintained that "[disinformation] . . . is false, incomplete, or misleading information that is passed, fed, or confirmed to a targetted individual, group, or country."[87] According to a KGB training manual, cited in a 1980 Congressional Report:[88]

> strategic disinformation assists in the execution of state tasks and is directed at misleading the enemy concerning basic questions of state policy, the military-economic status, and the scientific-technical achievements of the Soviet Union; the policy of certain imperialist states with respect to each other and other countries; and the specific counterintelligence tasks of the organs of state security.

While these definitions are helpful, they also have shortcomings. Both the CIA and the KGB statements, for example, imply that disinformation always is composed of information which is false. However, according to Ladislav Bittman (a former Czechoslovak intelligence officer who specialized in disinformation operations), the message may contain "both true and false information, leaked to an opponent to deceive him." Bittman further asserts that the target of disinformation is "the decision-makers . . . rather than the public at large."[89] Some analysts dispute this latter point, arguing that the target is sometimes a mass audience. Other observers take a much broader approach. They define disinformation as any government communication (either overt or covert) containing intentionally false and misleading material, often combined selectively with true information, which seeks to mislead and manipulate either elites or a mass audience.

While disinformation, in our view, may be either overt or covert, the present study is concerned only with disinformation that is conducted secretly. Covert disinformation is a non-attributed or falsely attributed communication, written or oral, containing intentionally false, incomplete, or misleading information (frequently combined with true information), which seeks to deceive, misinform, and/or mislead the target. Either foreign governmental and non-governmental elites, or a foreign mass audience, may comprise the target. In comparison with overt propaganda, covert disinformation usually is employed in a selective and discriminating manner. This technique may be advanced through rumors, forgeries, manipulative political actions, agents of influence, front organizations, and other means. The objective of disinformation is to lead the target to believe in the veracity of the material presented and consequently to act in the interests of the nation conducting the disinformation operation.

Agent-of-influence operations, another form of secret active measures emphasized in this book, are carried out by a person who subtly and artfully uses his or her position, influence, power, and credibility to promote the objectives of a foreign power in ways unattributable to that power. The general means of conducting these operations range from the utilization of a controlled agent of influence (someone who is recruited, and advances the interests of a foreign power in response to specific orders and direction) to the exploitation of an unwitting but manipulated individual. Between the controlled agent and the unwitting collaborator is the "trusted contact," a person who consciously advances the objectives of a foreign power, is in contact with that state regarding how to accomplish these goals, and may receive some form of assistance and reward for this collaboration. Unlike the controlled agent, however, the trusted contact is not formally recruited, does not receive precise orders, and is not under tight direction. The Soviets appear to employ all three of these variations.

The agent of influence may engage in disinformation and/or covert propaganda. A journalist writing for a Western news-paper with a large circulation, for example, would likely be involved in covert propaganda efforts on behalf of Moscow. This same journalist also could be involved in disinformation activities. Moscow may feed the agent information which inten-tionally seeks to deceive and mislead readers, associates, or government leaders.

Our study of secret political techniques also focuses on covert propaganda. In contrast to its overt counterpart, covert propaganda emanates from a falsely attributed or non-attributed channel. Various mass media channels can be used to dissemi-nate covert propaganda, including campaigns orchestrated in the world press by journalists acting as agents of influence, clandes-tine radio broadcasts, and the propaganda activities of interna-tional front organizations.[90]

In Chapter IV, specific Soviet covert active measures in each of these categories will be studied. The specific operations examined include Soviet manipulation of a major international front organization (covert propaganda and disinformation); a lengthy Soviet agent-of-influence operation (covert propaganda and disinformation); and examples of Soviet forgeries (disinfor-mation). Chapter V contains interviews with former Soviet bloc intelligence officers who specialized in these covert activities in the early 1960s and the late 1970s.

The General Objectives of Overt Propaganda and Covert Political Techniques

A review of the relevant Western literature published in the 1950s and the 1960s yields alternative explanations regarding the purposes of these activities. However, even though these studies focused on a variety of Soviet campaigns conducted at different times, a number of scholars have reached similar conclusions.[91]

While the content of particular themes has changed to reflect the issues and events of the day, the principal goals of Soviet overt propaganda and covert political techniques have remained consistent—to weaken the United States and NATO; and to extol the achievements of the Soviet Union, thereby creating a favorable environment for the advancement of Moscow's objectives. The literature suggests that Soviet leaders have hoped to achieve the following specific aims through the use of propaganda and political warfare.

1. To influence American, European, and world public opinion to believe that US military and political policies are the major cause of international conflict and crisis.

2. To demonstrate that the United States is an aggressive, militaristic, and imperialistic power.

3. To isolate the United States from its friends and allies (especially those in NATO), and to discredit those states which cooperate with the United States.

4. To discredit the US and NATO military and intelligence establishments.

5. To demonstrate that the policies and objectives of the United States are incompatible with those of the underdeveloped nations.

6. To confuse world public opinion concerning Soviet global ambitions, creating a favorable environment for Soviet foreign policy.

The remainder of this study examines the overt propaganda and covert political techniques that Moscow directed at the United States and NATO during the 1960–1980 period to determine how closely these measures conformed to the above-described thematic objectives.

CHAPTER III

SOVIET OVERT PROPAGANDA THEMES, 1960–1980

SOVIET EXTERNAL PROPAGANDA usually seeks to portray the USSR as a near-perfect society. It praises those foreign governments and movements that support Soviet policies and objectives, and excoriates those which oppose them. The preponderance of this propaganda is directed against the United States, its NATO allies, and other nations friendly to these countries.[1] Soviet commentary on international affairs emanates from multiple sources; and the high degree of consistency and coordination which characterizes this enormous outpouring indicates the extent to which the Soviet media support Moscow's objectives.[2] The close relationship between Soviet propaganda and Soviet foreign policy (i.e., between what is said and what is done) is impressive.

RESEARCH METHOD AND DESIGN

The vehicles of mass communications utilized by a government provide a data base for examining the country's internal and external preoccupations. During World War II, for example, the military and intelligence agencies of the Allied countries monitored enemy newspapers and radio stations, and counts were made of various kinds of substantive references. Variations in the number of such references from week to week provided clues to enemy morale, intentions, and actions. This information then was used in Allied war planning.[3]

Building on this experience, social scientists in recent decades have studied mass communications systematically in order to gain insights into the politics and culture of various nation-states. This extensive body of literature, which cuts across the social science disciplines, is too large to review here.[4] However, by examining the kinds of research issues addressed in these various studies of mass communications, it is possible to develop a classification of research questions relevant to the study of foreign propaganda. Our own project has been guided by these questions.[5]

In conjunction with these research developments, analysts increasingly have utilized a special research method—quantitative content analysis—to examine systematically the substance of mass communications.[6] While the scrutiny of such records is not new, this approach is an attempt to analyze methodically the content of communications data over a specified period of time, through designated means of classification and statistical tabulation. In comparison with previous methods, content analysis proceeds under specific rules or controls that render it more systematic and objective.[7]

While quantitative content analysis has its advantages, it also has weaknesses. Specifically, primary concern with quantification may overshadow the importance of the insights and judgments which might be drawn from a textual analysis of the substance of a particular communication.[8] To overcome this shortcoming, this study combines quantitative content analysis with descriptive textual analysis. This allows for the identification, classification, and quantification of major thematic trends, and produces a more substantive and in-depth analysis of the content and focus of Soviet foreign propaganda. The initiation of such an approach begins with the selection of a credible source (newspaper, radio broadcast, etc.), the time period to be examined, and the unit of measurement.

First, the most desirable media source—determined to be the one characterized by the greatest degree of authoritativeness and regularity—was sought as the data base for the conduct of quantitative content analysis. While certain Soviet media sources are considered more authoritative than others, it was necessary to take into account other factors as well. Quantitative content analysis also requires a source that appears with a sufficient degree of regularity. Additionally, given the modest resources available for this study, it was crucial that the source not be too voluminous. Finally, it was necessary that the source be focused exclusively on international affairs, and be designed for reading by foreign audiences. It is important to note that the nature and content of Soviet propaganda may vary, depending on the target audience. Significant differences often exist between propaganda which is directed at both internal and external audiences, and that which is intended strictly for export.

The source selected for the quantitative content analysis of Soviet foreign propaganda efforts during the 1960–1980 period was the weekly "International Review" column in *Pravda*. This commentary (generally appearing on page 4, covering a third of the page) focuses on international affairs; is published in a highly authoritative newspaper (intended for both domestic and foreign audiences); has appeared regularly since 1967 (generally on Sunday), and appeared fairly regularly prior to that time; and provides a sample which is manageable for our research purposes. Whereas other sources were considered, none satisfied the requirements identified above as adequately as did "International Review."[9] Of course, all quantitative analyses are accompanied by their own particular limitations, and the present case is no exception.[10]

With respect to the descriptive textual analysis, the source selected was the weekly Soviet foreign affairs magazine, *New Times*. This publication covers basically the same themes as the "International Review" column but in much greater detail, and appears to be designed primarily for foreign audiences. *New Times* apparently also is used for internal propaganda purposes. A broader and more general treatment of a given issue is presented in "International Review," which—as a result of the authoritativeness it carries—serves to establish the official Soviet perspective on the subject. In this study, the textual analysis of *New Times* was undertaken to determine whether the messages carried in one source focusing on both internal and external audiences (i.e., "International Review") are closely associated with those of another source which appears to be directed primarily at foreign targets (i.e., *New Times*). Additionally, an examination of *New Times* allows for an observation of the ways in which a briefer commentary carried in "International Review" may be developed and amplified in another publication.

In sum, quantitative content analysis of *Pravda*'s "International Review" combined with textual analysis of *New Times* provides a systematic means for examining the twenty-year Soviet propaganda campaign directed against the United States and NATO during the period under study in this book. This research approach yields two kinds of findings, which are analyzed in the remainder of this chapter.[11] The quantitative content analysis of "International Review" has made possible the classification of Soviet propaganda messages directed at the United States and NATO into ten thematic categories. These ten themes are ranked on the basis of the relative frequency (measured in percentages) with which each theme appeared during a series of twelve-week intervals occurring in the years 1960–1962, 1967–1969, and 1976–1979. The frequency scores are plotted on trend line graphs according to a method known as longitudinal analysis, which allows the frequency of appearance of various themes to be compared during segments of the 1960–1980 time period. The textual analysis of *New Times*, for its part, has resulted in a detailed description and explanation of the range of issues presented in this Soviet media source during the years between 1960 and 1980.

GENERAL PROPAGANDA THEMES

Quantitative content analysis of *Pravda*'s "International Review" during the 1960–1980 period has identified ten general propaganda themes related to the United States and NATO. These ten themes (listed below) constitute the principal ways in which the West was characterized throughout this rather large data base. The findings of this quantitative analysis also have been corroborated by our textual analysis of *New Times*.

Themes	Key Terms Reflecting These Themes
1. *Aggressiveness*	*Adventurist, provocative, increasing international tensions, aggressive, interfering in or exploiting the developing world.* Although most Soviet references to aggressiveness singled out the United States, the proportion of references to aggressiveness which referred to the West as a whole (or to NATO, capitalism, imperialism, or specific NATO countries) increased during the two decades under study. During 1960–1962, 75 percent of "International Review" references to aggressiveness singled out the United States. During 1967–1969 and 1976–1979, the figures were 60 percent and 55 percent, respectively.
2. *Militarism*	*Militaristic, promoting arms races, seeking military superiority, promoting the Cold War, employing force.*

During 1960–1962, 75 percent of all references to militarism singled out the United States. With respect to the NATO allies, West German revanchism frequently was described as driving the Federal Republic toward military expansionism. During 1976–1979, militarism again was a prominent theme, with 55 percent of these references directed at the United States. When references were directed at Europe, the NATO military leadership most frequently was singled out.

3. *Opposition to Negotiations*

Opposed to negotiated settlement of international issues, opposed to detente and the Strategic Arms Limitation Talks (SALT), against East-West cooperation.

Opposition to negotiations became a major theme during the late 1970s, when 70 percent of all references to this theme singled out the United States. This theme first appeared in 1962. Prior to that time, attention was focused on various Soviet proposals for disarmament, rather than on American intransigence.

4. *Crisis in the West*

Political, economic, or social crises or contradictions in Western societies.

During the 1960s, the United States was identified in about half of these references. In the 1976–1979 period, as references of this sort increased, only about 25 percent were directed at the United States, while European nations—both individually and as a group—received increasing coverage.

5. *Threatening Communist Bloc Unity*

Attempting to subvert Communist unity, interfering in the affairs of Communist states, conducting anti-Soviet propaganda and political actions.

With the exception of the period surrounding the 1968 Czech crisis, these references were minimal during the 1960s. During 1976–1979 this became an important theme, with 55 percent of all references of this sort identifying the United States.

6. *Realism*

Favoring detente and negotiations with the USSR, having a positive attitude about the Communist bloc, favoring peace and arms reductions.

Only during 1976–1979 did references to "realism" reach a significant level. These references usually took the form of identifying certain individuals or groups in the United States or the NATO countries who were seen to hold so-called realistic (i.e., cooperative) attitudes.

7. *NATO Alliance Problems*

Disunity, contradictions within the Western alliance, US interference in the affairs of Europe.

Although it was a minor theme in each of the three periods examined, this theme received increasing attention during 1976–1979.

8. *US Unreliability*

Existence of two contradictory tendencies in American foreign policy (aggressiveness and "realism").

This theme did not appear during the 1960s, and was only a minor theme during 1976–1979. When these references did appear during the latter period, it was usually in conjunction with one of the other themes listed above.

9. *Collusion with Another Soviet Enemy*

Collusion between the United States and/or NATO and another Soviet enemy.

This was a minor theme during 1960–1962, and virtually disappeared during 1967–1969. It reappeared in 1976–1979, with most references directed at Sino-American negotiations.

10. *Human Rights Violations*

Human rights violations in the West, principally in the United States.

A very minor theme during the entire period, with peak emphasis occurring during 1977.

DESCRIPTIVE ANALYSIS OF SOVIET FOREIGN PROPAGANDA THEMES DIRECTED AGAINST THE UNITED STATES AND NATO

Period One: 1960–1962

The main thrust of the Soviet propaganda directed against the United States and NATO during the years 1960–1962 concentrated on American aggressiveness, militarism, and sabotage of Soviet peace and disarmament proposals. During the first half of the period, the Soviets in various publications emphasized the sincerity and depth of their commitment to disarmament and peace objectives.[12] Numerous articles appeared describing in detail various Soviet disarmament plans. In January 1960, for example, *New Times* praised the CPSU proposal for immediate "general and complete disarmament,"[13] and emphasized how both the USSR and the West would benefit economically from a reduction in weaponry appropriations.[14] This theme served as the cornerstone of Khrushchev's January 1960 report to the Supreme Soviet. *New Times* and *Pravda* then used the report as the basis for various stories extolling the Soviet disarmament effort.

In actuality, Soviet use of "peace" as a major theme is part of a much older propaganda effort.[15] According to Barghoorn, over the years Soviet "determination to exploit the world's longing for peace as a propaganda weapon has been reflected in myriad ways. The peace theme is injected into almost every aspect of Soviet propaganda."[16] This began as early as 1922, when G. V. Chicherin, Soviet Commissar of Foreign Affairs, submitted to the Genoa conference the first of a seemingly unending series of proposals for immediate and general disarmament. For the next forty years, Moscow conducted an unrelenting and many-sided campaign centered around the world disarmament cause.[17] Thus, in contrast to the connotation carried by the Western concept of peace, as reflected in the Charter of the United Nations,[18] the Soviets view peace as a valuable weapon of political warfare for use against the non-Communist world.[19]

If Soviet propaganda portrays the USSR as the champion of peace and disarmament, the United States and its NATO allies (especially Britain) have been depicted as the major obstacles to the implementation of Soviet proposals.[20] On August 15, 1960, *Pravda* referred to "aggressive circles in the US and other Western countries" which were behind this obstructionist policy.[21] *New Times* carried similar charges, but went further in developing the theme by identifying specific groups in the

United States which were preventing disarmament. Specifically, forces within the Pentagon and the so-called military-industrial complex (M-I-C) were seen as responsible, through their active promotion of nuclear testing, increased defense spending, the stockpiling of nuclear weapons, and such provocative acts as Francis Gary Powers' U-2 overflight of the Soviet Union which sabotaged the May 1960 Paris summit.[22]

The United States also was charged with distorting Soviet disarmament proposals and making unreasonable negotiating demands. A case in point was Washington's pressure during the 1961 nuclear test ban talks in Geneva for an on-site inspection stipulation. *New Times* commentary stated:[23]

> The new US administration has, judging by all the signs, only partially departed from the absurd and unacceptable proposals of the Eisenhower government. It has made no constructive steps toward the Soviet position.... Suffice to say the US demands unconditional Soviet consent to twenty inspections a year and, moreover, by teams composed entirely of foreign personnel. Another US demand is that all control posts in the USSR be headed by foreigners.... All evidence shows that Soviet concessions made possible a compromise settlement.... The Western powers, however, rejected the proposal....

Throughout the 1960–1962 period, Soviet propaganda attempted to utilize the disarmament issue to isolate the United States from its allies. However, when compared with the harshness of the Soviet attack against the United States mounted after mid-1961, Soviet commentary during the earlier portion of this period was marked by a degree of restraint.[24] Beginning in the latter half of 1961, as tensions between Washington and Moscow escalated over Berlin and other issues, *Pravda* presented a much more negative characterization of American intentions. The United States now was portrayed as obstructing disarmament for more sinister but ideologically discernible reasons.[25] This shift in themes was apparent in a September 13,

1961 *New Times* article which asserted that "the United States and its allies are gearing their war machine to ever higher speeds, carrying the arms drive to unprecedented portions ... bringing international tensions to a fever pitch."[26]

By the end of the year, the "capitalist world" was charged with unleashing "a frenzied arms race and extensive war preparation. Inflated military expenditures in the imperialist countries, notably the United States, have risen sharply. War planners are working at top speed."[27] Moscow further asserted that the United States was "raring for a fight":[28]

> That nuclear-armed imperialism presents great danger is beyond doubt. That imperialism looks to the future with fear is beyond doubt too. Like all social forces condemned by history, it convulsively clings to the old and seeks to erect every conceivable obstacle to progress. . . . Imperialism is sterile. It is afraid to look into the future, for the future is Communism. . . . The changeover from one social system to another is a law of history.

During 1962, these charges became increasingly acrimonious. While Moscow continued to propose new disarmament plans,[29] and described through articles on Hiroshima the horrors that a nuclear war would produce,[30] Soviet propaganda now claimed that US military planners sought to develop a first-strike, nuclear warfighting doctrine and capability. This theme appeared in a March 21, 1962 article in *New Times* entitled "Acceptable Nuclear War—The Latest US Theory." According to the author, Major-General Teplimsky, US civilian strategists "cynically justify an American first strike" on the grounds that "it would lead to the elimination of the evil enemy ... to secure that liquidation at almost any price is worthwhile."[31] Teplimsky went on to assert that this first-strike strategy constituted an integral feature of the Kennedy doctrine of flexible response.[32] The same issue of *New Times* contained an essay describing Moscow's vigorous pursuit of a "world without weapons."[33]

Throughout 1962, this thematic pattern—i.e., the USSR seeks a nuclear-free world,[34] while the United States actively works to develop a first-strike, nuclear warfighting capability—unfolded in a number of ways. For instance, the United States was charged with attempting to militarize space;[35] creating a doctrine of escalation control that includes the use of chemical and biological weapons, which Washington asserts are "humane weapons";[36] and proposing disarmament plans whose real purpose is to "undermine the Soviet defense system."[37] The principal architect of these policies was identified as the Secretary of Defense, Robert McNamara, who was characterized by Soviet propaganda as "America's Nuclear Napoleon."[38]

Soviet propaganda also advanced the theme of American aggressiveness and militarism by charging the United States with responsibility for a number of international crises that occurred during the 1960–1962 period. Both *Pravda* and *New Times* focused on events in Cuba, the Congo, Laos, Vietnam, and Berlin, to name the most prominent examples.[39] Directly associated with these charges were allegations of expanding US imperialism in the Third World. During the years spanning 1960 to 1962, the Congo, Vietnam, and Laos received growing attention. In 1960, for instance, a *New Times* article presented the South Vietnamese government as the patron of an imperialistic United States, which was portrayed as having undertaken a policy of arming and training South Vietnam's repressive military and security forces.[40]

This theme was amplified further during 1961, culminating in 1962 with the publication in *New Times* of a lengthy four-part series by journalist Wilfred Burchett, a long-time member of the Australian Communist Party.[41] Included among the many accusations levied against the United States in this series was the charge that American forces were using chemical and biological weapons in South Vietnam.[42] According to Burchett, "Using Asians as victims for tests of new weapons fits an all too familiar picture which stretches from Hiroshima."[43] (It is interesting to note that as a correspondent in North Korea during the Korean War, Burchett levied similar charges against the United States.[44])

In addition to Soviet propaganda concentrating on American aggressiveness, militarism, and sabotage of Soviet peace and disarmament initiatives, *Pravda* and *New Times* also carried a number of articles focusing on issues related to the character of, and problems concerning, the NATO alliance and its constituent states. While these latter issues received less coverage in *Pravda* than did those themes described above, the same was not true of *New Times*. Generally, coverage of NATO-related issues during the 1960–1962 segment focused on the threat of German revanchism and on alleged US domination and manipulation of the alliance.

The theme of German revanchism was utilized in a number of ways, with the apparent purpose in mind of splitting NATO by presenting West Germany as a serious threat to peace in Europe. Soviet propaganda claimed, for example, that leading figures in the government of Chancellor Konrad Adenauer were former key henchmen for Hitler. Perhaps the most publicized case was that of Adenauer's State Secretary, Dr. Hans Globke. According to *New Times*, Globke—in contrast to Bonn's argument that he was a "humble Ministry lawyer" who tried to incorporate legal constraints into the Nuremberg Laws—in reality was a major architect of the "Final Solution." A 1962 article stated:[45]

> Globke attended to the "legal" aspects of the plan—Eichmann directed its practical execution. Every occupied country at once came under the operation of the "Nuremberg Laws," which first robbed millions of people of their rights and led them to their death. . . . Globke determined who had to be massacred.
>
> But it was not only the Jews that the Nazis' racist policies set out to annihilate. They went much further. The "final solution" was to be applied to a number of other peoples too, notably the Slavs.

The article concluded by asserting that those who put Globke in power now were attempting to persuade Israel to "restrict publicity in the Eichmann case," out of fear Eichmann would expose other war criminals holding important positions in Adenauer's government.[46]

This attention to West German officials was associated

directly with Moscow's explanation of the motivations under-lying Bonn's revanchism and militarism. In a 1960 *New Times* article, Adenauer and his Defense Minister, Franz-Josef Strauss, were presented as the architects of a plan to resurrect the Wehrmacht under the guise of the Bundeswehr:[47]

> The West German Bundeswehr, organized and led by the militarists who were allowed to remain at large as a result of Western policy, are now back in the saddle. The Western powers . . . encouraged the revival of German imperialism, with the result that today its might has reached a point where it lays claim to a dominant role in capitalist Europe.

The article went on to warn that "what Bonn revenge-mongers want is war, not peace."[48] According to another *New Times* commentary, Strauss—to carry out this plan—had created an army of several million men, which was "becoming a menace to Europe's peace, and therewith to the German people them-selves."[49]

With this military capability, Adenauer and Strauss would be ready to unveil their true plans, which Moscow outlined in the following terms. Their "interest," stated a 1960 *New Times* essay, "is the swallowing up of [East Germany], forcibly destroying the socialist system . . . seizure of the Polish terri-tories east of the Oder, a new assault on Austria, on Czechoslovakia. . . . German reunion . . . is nothing but a pre-lude to revanche."[50]

Throughout 1960, 1961, and 1962, a number of articles predicted that the consequence of this rearmament would be a new imperial reich that would plunge all Europe into a devastat-ing war. Further, Soviet propagandists warned, if West Germany were to obtain a nuclear capability—a policy Bonn was por-trayed as actively pursuing under NATO auspices—the results for Europe would be catastrophic.[51] How likely was it that these dire developments would occur? According to a *New Times* article published in August 1960, Adenauer had successfully manipulated NATO into "encouraging West German rearmament," and Bonn already was using this outcome to embark on a "secret" remilitarization that would result in its "dominance in NATO . . . making that war bloc an instrument of its aggressive policy."[52]

Other variations on the West German issue also were presented in *Pravda* and *New Times* as a part of Moscow's campaign to split the NATO alliance. For instance, West Germany was depicted as secretly orchestrating a Europe-wide Fascist resurgence.[53] How did the United States fit into this scheme? What *Pravda* called "the close union of the most reactionary and aggressive American circles with West German militarist-revanchists" repeatedly received coverage during the 1960–1962 years.[54]

According to Moscow, this device was but one of a number of measures undertaken by the United States to manipulate and control NATO for its own ends. Additionally, the United States was seen as guilty of using West Berlin "as a source of tension and conflict, transforming it into a military base."[55] Whatever variation was used, however, the Soviet explanation of the underlying American purpose remained the same: i.e., the United States sought to enlist NATO behind its aggressive and militaristic policy of imperialism. Throughout this period, Moscow continually warned Europe that the United States was dragging it down a "dangerous and slippery path of warlike gambles."[56]

Finally, but to a lesser extent, Soviet propaganda also singled out the CIA for special attention (although the coverage during these years was not nearly so extensive as it would be during the 1976–1979 period). Between 1960 and 1962, *New Times* published articles on CIA global espionage programs and its alleged manipulation of the Peace Corps, a piece on CIA activities in West Germany, and an article purporting to show how the US Congress has no influence, let alone control, over any activities conducted by the CIA.[57] In the latter case, the author used statements allegedly made by Senator Wayne Morse to explain to the reader that the American "constitution provides that no government agency . . . shall be exempt from control of the Senate. But the CIA is completely exempt."[58] Little commentary was published during this time segment on the domestic policies of the United States or its NATO allies (with the exception of West Germany and France). However, a few articles did appear each year on the worsening crisis of world capitalism.[59]

Period Two: 1967–1969

Soviet overt propaganda during the 1967–1969 period continued to focus on allegations of American and NATO aggressiveness. However, these years also were characterized by some new tendencies not apparent during the earlier period discussed above. To begin with, while the theme of US aggressiveness continued to predominate, the number of secondary issues addressed by the Soviets increased throughout this time segment. Second, whereas the major issue employed during the 1960–1962 years to signify American aggressiveness was nuclear policy, emphasis on the Vietnam War now came to play this role (although nuclear policy did continue to receive coverage). A third change was related to what the Soviets term *kombinatsia*: during this period, an increasing Soviet effort to combine various questions and interrelate these issues in conjunction with general themes was apparent. Finally, at the end of this time segment, the first signs of the detente theme began to emerge.

The coverage devoted during these years to the involvement of the United States in the Vietnam War exceeded by far the attention paid to any other issue.[60] Soviet handling of the theme took a variety of forms, and focused on both the domestic and the international problems faced by the United States as a result of its role in the conflict. To begin with, Washington was charged with the initiation of a reckless and increasingly genocidal policy. During 1967, for instance, *New Times* accused the Pentagon of "trying to make good its failure in South Vietnam by stepping up its barbarous air war. . . . American planes bomb dykes and other irrigation installations which can in no way be called military objectives."[61]

Wartime activities were characterized as the outcome of a systematically planned and directed Pentagon policy. As stated in *New Times*, "the US command has deliberately timed these raids to coincide with the rise in the level of Vietnam rivers . . . to cause floods and destroy crops."[62] According to Soviet propaganda, the United States was guilty of the same kinds of atrocities for which the Nazis had been tried and convicted at Nuremberg.[63] In sum, America was characterized as the "War Society," guided by a "Napalm Morality."[64] Through the course of the 1967–1969 period, these charges became more virulent in tone.

What motivating forces underlay the decision of the United States to pursue such a policy? According to Moscow, US actions were the result of American imperialism and neocolonialism. "The Washington policy aims at making the Asian countries one vast colony of US imperialism in partnership with its European and Asian allies," asserted a writer in *New Times*. This policy will "doom Asia to remain the backwoods of the world, a raw material producing appendage to the imperialists. . . . The monopoly exploitation of the natural wealth of these countries block[s] the development of their natural industrial potential."[65]

In contrast to the portrayal of the United States as a government motivated by these malevolent forces, North Vietnam and the Viet Cong were presented as entities fighting for a just cause—Freedom, Independence, and Liberation—in the name of the Vietnamese people. This distinction, according to Moscow, served to explain why America was losing in Vietnam. An article in *New Times* stated: "The huge American war machine has proved incapable of smashing the enemies' resistence. . . . They are determined to go on fighting for their freedom and independence."[66]

This argument was amplified even more stridently during the Tet Offensive:[67]

> Nothing can bring the Vietnamese people to their knees. There is no military solution for Washington. The greater the scale of the aggression, the heavier the defeats inflicted on the aggressors. These are the home truths

made plain once again with renewed force by the patriotic forces against enemy-held South Vietnamese towns and US military bases.

Virtually the whole country is now the battle front. The US invaders have no rear areas left. . . . Vietnamese soil is burning under the aggressors' feet as all sections of the population—from peasants and workers to tradesmen and factory owners—are joining the fight. . . .

Indeed, what better illustration could there be of the fallacy of the escalation theory (US policy) than the capture by the guerrillas of the US embassy and government buildings in Saigon. . . . The USA has met with a political fiasco and is sustaining heavy defeats on the battlefield. The latest events make it plainer than ever.

Moscow's assertions that the Tet Offensive constituted an overwhelming success appear to have been part of a larger North Vietnamese propaganda effort, designed to promote the view that since the American military policy of 1965 to 1968 had failed to prevent this "devastating" countrywide offensive, the United States in effect had lost the war. In the Soviet view, the Tet Offensive now compelled the United States to turn to peace talks as Washington's only way out of the war.[68]

Soviet propaganda also concentrated increasingly on the effects within the United States of the Vietnam War, focusing on various domestic economic and political problems. Especially close (and supportive) attention was paid to the development of the American anti-war movement.[69] Racial tensions afflicting American cities also were given special emphasis, and were discussed as an important indicator of the demise of the American capitalist regime, as well as in connection with the Vietnam War. As *New Times* asserted in August 1967, "desperation accumulated through the decades and multiplied by bitter disappointment with the policies of the Johnson Administration once so lavish with its promises to the Negroes, is what makes the present racial conflict so sharp and irreconcilable."[70] While these developments were "aggravated by the war in Vietnam," the situation also was greatly exacerbated, in the view of the author, by "US reactionaries . . . who know no other way of solving racial problems than through fascist type terror and violence."[71]

During this period, the Soviets thus worked to combine the issues of the Vietnam War and America's domestic racial tensions (termed "Washington's Other War") into a general theme of the United States as "the War Society."[72] According to an August 1967 article in *New Times* entitled "A Sick Society," the United States was engaged in "waging two wars—at home against the Negroes and overseas, against Vietnam. . . . Both wars and both problems are closely interlinked," and are the result of "brute force American imperialism."[73]

Only twice during this three-year period did any other issue treated in *Pravda*'s "International Review" approach a level of coverage comparable to that accorded the Vietnam War. The first instance occurred as a result of the 1967 war in the Middle East; and during the latter half of 1967, the Middle East and Vietnam received approximately the same degree of emphasis. What, according to Moscow, was the role played by the United States in the 1967 war? Commentary in "International Review" asserted that while Israel was the aggressor, the United States (and Britain) were the motivating forces behind the scene.[74] *New Times* approached the issue in a similar fashion. Note, for example, how this publication described US and British opposition to a UN Security Council resolution condemning Israel:[75]

> The world has witnessed a new act of aggression; Israel was again the shock force, but there is not the slightest doubt the imperialist forces in the United States and Britain are behind it. It is not by chance that the US and British diplomats did their utmost to whitewash Israel when they opposed the adoption of a Security Council resolution condemning the aggressor. . . . There are many facts proving beyond all doubts that Israel and its Western backers were once again in league with one another.

As in the case of US involvement in Vietnam, American military assistance and support for Israel were characterized in Soviet propaganda as resulting from the requirements of imperialism. Specific US goals were said to include ensuring access to Persian Gulf oil and freedom of navigation in the Aqaba Gulf, as well as bringing about the overthrow of the Egyptian and Syrian governments. Regarding the Cairo and Damascus regimes, the American objective—according to Moscow—was to strike a blow against Third World "national liberation and revolutionary forces" (a major threat to imperialism) by toppling two of the major proponents of these struggles.[76]

The only other issue which received a level of coverage in *Pravda* during this period equal to the Vietnam War was related to the Soviet invasion of Czechoslovakia. Commentary in "International Review" charged the United States and other NATO members with attempting in connection with the Czech situation to subvert Communist bloc unity through the vehicle of malicious propaganda. Western methods were said to include the promotion of "counterrevolutionary" activities distorting the meaning of Soviet involvement in Czechoslovakia, and capitalizing on the crisis to give new stimulus to the Western arms buildup and to aggravate the situation in Europe.[77]

The 1967 war in the Middle East and the 1968 crisis in Czechoslovakia also received attention in *New Times* during these years, but this organ continued to stress two other issues which had been featured prominently during the 1960–1962 time segment: nuclear weapons policy and disarmament, and relations between the United States and its NATO allies. (While these themes also were discussed in "International Review," the coverage therein was not nearly so extensive as that found in *New Times*.)

In the case of Soviet propaganda focusing on NATO relations, Moscow continued to handle issues and developments in a manner designed to promote splits in the Western alliance. Specific attention was paid to the dangers of German revanchism, Bonn's goal of military domination of NATO, and Washington's manipulation of the alliance for purposes of achieving its own expansive ambitions.

A major line of attack stressed the dangers deriving from US cooperation with German revanchists, especially in connection with the strengthening of German military power. These developments, Moscow argued, posed a grave danger to the rest of Europe. An August 1967 "International Review" column, for example, accused "American Imperialists" of attempting to transform Europe into an "arena of aggression" in cooperation with West German revanchists, who are "dying to obtain both the dominant position in NATO and nuclear weapons" in the hope of realizing their World War II goals.[78] This column was typical of the general Soviet line set forth throughout the period. A *New Times* article entitled "Bundeswehr Over NATO," also published in August 1967, asserted that American-backed "revanchist schemes" of Adenauer and Strauss sought to "capture the key positions in NATO, establish its [West Germany's] supremacy in Western Europe, get its hands on the military (especially weapons of mass destruction) and economic resources of the entire West, and then set about executing Bonn's strategic design."[79]

As noted earlier in this chapter, West Germany's current "strategic design" was characterized by the Kremlin as nothing short of the plans entertained previously by "Hitler and his clique."[80] As was stated in a 1969 *New Times* article:[81]

> The West German government's program for revenge and revision of Europe's frontiers is there for all to see. It was drawn up by Franz-Josef Strauss, who in the early forties was a propaganda officer in Hitler's Wehrmacht and in the latter established himself as a protege of the Americans in West German politics. . . . "Our task today," says Strauss, "should be to create a belt between Russia and Western Europe, a kind of 'buffer Europe'" to consist of "Poland, Czechoslovakia, Hungary, Bulgaria, Romania, etc." . . . Bonn is preparing the ground for war against the East in every possible manner: militarily, psychologically, ideologically.

In addition to accusations of revanchism, Soviet propaganda also levied the charge of neo-fascism against the West German government. As was the case in the 1960–1962 period, the Kremlin's objective was to convince the Europeans that German ambitions gravely threatened the security of all Europe.

A second line of Soviet verbal assault against NATO concentrated directly on the United States. In addition to the claim that Washington was promoting German revanchism, two other themes received considerable attention: the charge that the United States was orchestrating NATO's continuing military buildup, and the assertion that the nuclear component of NATO strategy (i.e., the American nuclear arsenal and doctrine) endangered the very existence of Europe. Moscow frequently warned that "the development of military technology and the saturation of the continent with weapons of mass destruction [by the United States] have reached a point where Europeans must give serious thought to the danger that faces them . . . the danger of turning Europe into the center of a nuclear war."[82]

In stressing this danger, the Soviets often made the point that many Europeans had awakened to the extreme danger American nuclear strategy posed for the continent.[83] For example, a 1969 article in *New Times* reported growing disillusionment with the American strategy of flexible response:[84]

> In Western Europe the new approach was assessed as an attempt on the part of the US military to take cover behind the backs of their NATO partners. The result was a growth of distrust and suspicion between the Atlantic partners. And although the "flexible response" strategy was eventually adopted, under pressure from Washington, as the common doctrine of NATO, this has not put an end to controversies.

By 1969, Soviet propaganda was proclaiming an ever-widening opposition to American nuclear strategy, and anti-NATO demonstrations in Europe were described as part of a rising tide of opposition to NATO's policy of "preparing for aggression."[85]

With respect to the theme of disarmament, *New Times*—and, to a lesser extent, "International Review"—continued to focus (as in the 1960–1962 period) on the Soviet commitment to arms control and world disarmament, even in light of the aggressive US nuclear warfighting strategy and war preparations noted above.[86] The Kremlin's charges that the United States was engaged in preparations to fight a nuclear war dovetailed with Moscow's characterizations of Washington's aggressive NATO strategy, and the two assertions in combination served to reinforce the portrayal of the United States as a government recklessly preparing to initiate a nuclear war.

During the final year of the 1967–1969 time segment, however, the Soviets undertook a partial shift of focus and began to suggest that detente between Moscow and Washington might be possible. In November 1969, the preparatory first round of SALT I began in Helsinki. Commentary appearing in "International Review" during the months leading up to the talks was cautious, but did suggest the possibility of limited Soviet-American cooperation on certain issues. The March 23, 1969 issue, for example, carried a discussion concerning the existence of "realistic" (i.e., cooperative) forces in the West.[87] By late 1969, such commentary had become more frequent. What, in the view of Moscow, were the forces which made this change possible? According to a December 1969 "International Review" column, the American defeat in Vietnam and Washington's increasing recognition of the strength of the Soviet military power had forced certain elements in the United States to come to grips with the limitations of American power and influence.[88]

Soviet propaganda pointed out, however, that whereas some circles favoring negotiations were active in the United States and Europe, other elements in the capitalist camp continued to use all possible means to escalate tension and conflict.[89] It was this latter group, the Soviets asserted, that was responsible for the promotion of German revanchism, the attempted manipulation of the Czech and Middle East crisis, and the escalation of the Vietnam War. Moscow in fact went so far as to suggest the existence of a grand conspiracy, in which these reactionary elements in the West had aligned themselves with the Communist Chinese in order to plot collectively against the Soviet Union. Soviet commentary regarding the Sino-Soviet fighting along the Ussuri River during the summer of 1969 provides a good example of Moscow's use of this theme. According to *Pravda*, the Chinese initiated the fighting in order to generate a reason for cooperation with the United States against the Soviet Union.[90]

An analysis of Soviet commentary appearing during the early 1970s is beyond the scope of this study. However, a cursory review of the issues of *New Times* published during these years indicates that the theme of American "realism" received increasing coverage as the rapprochement between the United States and the Soviet Union unfolded. In his recent book entitled *Dangerous Relations: The Soviet Union in World Politics*, Ulam describes insightfully Moscow's attitude toward and approach to detente, and the way in which detente influenced Soviet foreign policy behavior. Ulam notes that, on the one hand, leaders in the Kremlin had no expectations that detente might bring to an end the "struggle between two systems"; this would continue, although in less dangerous forms.[91] On the other hand, Ulam continues, the possibility of cooperation with Washington did lead to a modification in the tone used by Moscow in its commentary on the United States. With respect to Soviet press treatment of Nixon's foreign policy, Ulam observes that the Kremlin was:[92]

> careful not to permit any explicit criticism of its partner in detente—the Nixon Administration. On the contrary, the President and his advisers were praised for their statesmanship and realism, as exhibited both in their resolve and in their readiness to embark on a new type of relationship with Moscow and the entire Soviet bloc.

The Arab-Israel War of 1973, the Watergate scandal in Washington, Soviet involvement in Angola, and other disruptive events caused setbacks in the detente process as the decade progressed. However, as will be discussed in the next section of this chapter, the Soviet theme of realism reemerged later in the decade with the election of Jimmy Carter.

Period Three: 1976–1979

Soviet overt propaganda during the 1976–1979 period was characterized by both a continuation of certain tendencies from earlier time segments and the appearance of some new features. The number of issues examined continued to increase, although the degree of coverage granted to each varied widely. By the late 1970s, the extended coverage of one or two issues characteristic of the two earlier periods had been replaced by an examination of half a dozen subjects. In addition to increasing the number of issues covered, Moscow combined various issues and closely interrelated selected themes.

The issue of detente, which had first appeared in 1969, became a major theme during the late 1970s. In fact, one of the questions raised most persistently during these years was whether or not realism (i.e., detente with Moscow) could gain ascendancy over the aggressiveness and militarism that had dominated Western foreign policy throughout the post-World War II era. Both *Pravda*'s "International Review" and *New Times* closely followed detente-connected developments, and related their outcome to a number of other issues and events.

Soviet propaganda during the 1976–1979 period also demonstrated an improved capacity to respond immediately to crises and key events. Additionally, the language employed in Soviet propaganda—which was unoriginal, dull, and ritualistic (perhaps some of its major weaknesses) in the 1960s—had become considerably less unimaginative by the late 1970s.

An examination of commentary published during 1976 reveals a partial modification of the severe charges against the United States which had dominated earlier propaganda. Evident instead is cautious speculation regarding the prospects of detente, and emphasis on the central role played by Soviet peace and disarmament initiatives in the promotion of this rapprochement. In the spring of 1976, for instance, "International Review" affirmed Soviet enthusiasm for detente and Moscow's desire to improve relations with the West.[93] Other issues of *Pravda* pronounced detente to be the "leading goal of international life,"[94] and asserted that when the West recognized this fact, "agreements [would be] possible on even the most complex problems."[95]

The increasing coverage granted to the detente process in the West generally drew attention, however, to "two contradictory tendencies." While realistic forces supportive of detente were in evidence in the West, there also existed "opponents of detente" who sought to subvert the process.[96] Still, even given these negative forces, the Soviets suggested that the election of Jimmy Carter might "heighten the effectiveness of detente."[97]

During the first half of 1977, favorable references regarding the likelihood of detente continued to hold an important place in Soviet commentary, and various articles referred to the newly-inaugurated Carter Administration as the leading Western proponent of more "realistic" East-West relations. As early as December 1976, *New Times* observed that "several of President-elect James Carter's influential advisors on military and foreign affairs," as well as Carter himself, had spoken—in the words of *New Times*—of the "desirability of reducing dependence upon atomic weapons" and the need "to freeze, at the present level, the number of missiles, the number of warheads, overall throw weight, and qualitative status."[98]

After Carter entered the White House, Moscow continued to stress "his intention to work for the normalization of international relations and to end the stockpiling of nuclear weapons," as well as his desire to "reach a new agreement on the limitation of strategic arms."[99] It also was noted that "sober views of American-Soviet relations have been voiced by such influential members of the Carter Administration as Secretary of State Cyrus Vance and Secretary of Defense Harold Brown."[100] Outside the Administration, *New Times* pointed out, "George Kennan, author of containment based on the use of force" (among other figures) now was showing "a certain degree of realism."[101]

A similar trend was evident during this period in the Soviet approach to Europe. In June 1976, *Pravda* observed that "realistic political forces in West Europe know there is no alternative to detente."[102] The Soviet portrayal of the Bonn government during these years constituted a major reversal from the 1960s: rather than being presented as the principal opponent of detente, as might have been expected, West Germany now was characterized as the most realistic member of NATO. Hints of this change initially appeared in 1969, when Soviet commentary first identified the existence of "two contradictory tendencies" in West Germany.[103] By the latter half of the 1970s, charges of West German revanchism, neo-fascism, militarism, and nuclear ambitions rarely appeared.

The figure most frequently identified by Moscow as responsible for these favorable developments was Chancellor Helmut Schmidt.[104] In April 1978, *New Times* portrayed Schmidt as the architect of "treaties and agreements" with the Soviet Union intended to "create the basis for a long-term process of normalization."[105] Normalization of relations, according to Moscow, rapidly was becoming the "major aspect of the foreign policy of the West German coalition government."[106]

As noted above, Soviet commentary concerning realistic forces in the West always was discussed in terms of "two contradictory tendencies": i.e., while the forces of realism sought normalization of East-West relations, the Pentagon and the military-industrial complex (M-I-C) continually opposed any moves in this direction. During late 1976 and early 1977, Moscow asserted that the opponents of detente were preparing rapidly to sabotage the SALT II treaty and any other potential arms control agreements.[107]

According to Soviet commentary, these obstructionist forces were extremely influential and possessed great power. *New Times* credited "the war industry corporations and the military," for example, with having successfully pressured President Ford to "renounce the word [detente]" during the 1976 Presidential election campaign.[108] Since the election, the article continued, these forces had unleashed a "massive propaganda campaign in favor of increased appropriations for the Pentagon."[109] The major thrust of these "highly provocative reports," it was argued, was designed to misrepresent Soviet defense spending, military strength, and nuclear strategy. In the case of the latter, these reactionary elements had set forth the view that the Soviet Union actively planned to "strike the first blow." According to Moscow, such a plan constituted not the strategy of the Soviet Union, but rather that of the United States.[110]

Moscow was not satisfied to simply reject these charges as the same old fabrications (i.e., "The Old Bogey"). Additionally, Soviet leaders initiated a lengthy and vilifying campaign against the "Pentagon and military-industrial complex," with the apparent intention of placing complete responsibility for any escalation of international tensions or the arms race in the hands of these elements.[111] During 1976, New Times featured articles on such subjects as the "Death Merchants," which served as the title of a lengthy exposé of the alleged power and influence of the M-I-C.[112] During the first half of 1977, emphasis centered on US nuclear strategy and weapons development.

With respect to the former, it was claimed in Soviet commentary that the American posture had been based since the late 1940s on the twin goals of nuclear superiority and first-strike capacity.[113] Moscow's verbal assault against US weapons developments, for its part, concentrated on the Pentagon's so-called "humane weapon, the neutron bomb."[114] How powerful, in the view of the Kremlin, was this M-I-C/Pentagon coalition? Could it alter the direction of the Carter Administration policy? According to Soviet commentary, if Carter were to resist the pressures of this coalition, given the "unlimited power in the Pentagon . . . a military coup d'etat is no longer unthinkable."[115] Furthermore, noted New Times, such views are held by members of the US Congress.[116]

Attention also was devoted to similar forces within the NATO leadership which stood in opposition to detente. As a 1976 article in New Times asserted:[117]

> It has become clear why the NATO Supreme Commander is indulging in Dulles-like teetering on the brink. He is evidently alarmed by the fact that, in the atmosphere

of detente . . . West European allies are beginning to lose interest in the costly arms buildup and are declaring even more strongly for its limitation and even curtailment.

A *New Times* article published the next year noted that despite this popular trend, the NATO leadership persisted in vetoing agreements that would halt the arms race, justifying their actions "under the cover of fabrications about the 'Soviet threat.' "[118]

During the latter half of 1977, as—in the Soviet view—the forces of aggression and militarism began to assert themselves even more strongly in the United States, the tone of Soviet remarks concerning detente turned sharply pessimistic. Attention to American military developments now began to dominate Soviet commentary, with a special focus on the neutron weapon.[119] The Carter Administration was strongly berated for submitting to pressures from the M-I-C and the Pentagon for the deployment of new nuclear weapons and the establishment of a first-strike capability. *New Times* asserted:[120]

> President Carter has given the go-ahead for the manufacture of cruise missiles. Thus, the warnings at home and abroad about the grave dangers of deploying this strategic weapon have gone unheeded by the White House. . . . The decision on the mass production of cruise missiles creates a new situation, complicating still further the reaching of agreements at the Soviet-American strategic arms limitation talks. . . . Hardly a day passes without news from the arms market . . . the military budget has risen by $10,000 million. . . . Early in June, the President decided to deploy the new MK-12A nuclear warhead, to be installed on Minuteman-3 . . . the new warhead is directly related to the Pentagon's "first strike" concept. At the end of June, over a thousand million dollars were allocated for the so-called neutron bomb.

The author of this article concluded that "sober-minded Americans cannot but wonder where US policy is done—in the White House or in the Pentagon?"[121]

What, from Moscow's point of view, could account for Carter's vacillation? According to *New Times*, this policy shift was the result of a political backlash mounted by the extreme right, which had launched an offensive that "reveals their unscrupulous approach to key foreign policy issues."[122] Major players were said to include the M-I-C, the Pentagon, Congressional hawks, and such powerful "unofficial" groups as the Committee on the Present Danger.[123] Carter was criticized for "not making the slightest attempt to counter this malicious propaganda"; and his foreign policy, now described by Moscow as mirroring the program of the extreme right, was said to be "setting [the United States] on a dangerous course."[124]

During the months beginning in mid-1977 and continuing through 1978, Soviet propaganda concentrated on those forces within the United States and the NATO alliance which promoted a foreign policy of militarism and extremism, and on Carter's capitulation to these forces. This focus is apparent in the following excerpt from a lengthy *New Times* article entitled the "Military-Industrial Complex: Money, Arms, Power," published in May 1978.[125]

> The United States is the birthplace of the world's first and most powerful military-industrial complex. . . . It captured key positions in the country's economy and, like a cancerous tumor, infected the whole body of the state. . . . There is practically no sphere of activity by the state which is not influenced by the military-industrial complex. . . . The expansion of their war preparations adversely affects the solution of social and economic problems on a national and international scale. . . . The solution of these problems is usually postponed from year to year in the capitalist world because priority is given to the production of aircraft and missiles, tanks, and atomic missile carriers.

The author of this article goes on to explain that the M-I-C justifies its arms buildup through a "misinformation" offensive that "vehemently assails detente" through propagation of the

"Soviet threat bogey."[126] The article also identifies the Committee on the Present Danger as the unofficial lobby of the M-I-C, and a key promoter of "that tired old propaganda line that the USSR seeks world supremacy."[127] In Europe, *New Times* asserted further, the main center of the US military-industrial complex is found in the NATO headquarters in Brussels.[128]

Soviet commentary during the mid-1977 through 1978 time span linked these general charges of growing American militarism to various specific issues, the most important of which was the neutron weapon. During the summer of 1977, soon after the US Congress had approved funding for the weapon, the Soviets unleashed a massive propaganda campaign designed to marshal international opinion against the decision of the Carter Administration to deploy the armament. Within a few months, the neutron weapon had become a major political issue in virtually every European capital. Although Moscow's campaign in and of itself was brief in duration, it did constitute in effect still another phase in the post-World War II Soviet propaganda effort directed at the misrepresentation of US/NATO deployment decisions and defense appropriations.

The objectives of the Soviet anti-neutron campaign were to halt NATO's deployment of the weapon, and divide the alliance by presenting the United States as the architect of a defense policy that would lead to war in Europe. In many respects, this campaign was a replay of an effort mounted during 1961 and 1962, when the possibility of developing such a device initially was discussed in the West. At that time, the Soviets—recognizing the important contribution the neutron weapon could make to the defense of Western Europe—initiated immediately a propaganda offensive against development of the armament. According to Khrushchev, "the neutron bomb as conceived by American scientists should kill everything living but leave material assets intact. . . . They are acting as robbers who want to murder a man without staining his suit with blood so as to be able to use his suit."[129]

Over a decade and a half later, Soviet propaganda reproduced in almost exactly the same configuration the charges levied by Khrushchev in the early 1960s. The neutron weapon now was described as a capitalist weapon designed expressly to destroy living things while leaving property intact, and was portrayed as an inhumane armament which produces a death more horrible than that caused by any other weapon. Moscow asserted as well that the neutron weapon would lower the threshold of nuclear war, thereby rendering nuclear conflict more "thinkable" and more likely. Further, it was claimed, since the weapon was intended primarily for use in Western Europe, the European people thus would become the first victims of a nuclear war directed by the United States. Finally, the Soviets argued that deployment of the neutron weapon would disturb nuclear military parity between the United States and the Soviet Union, thereby escalating the arms race.[130] In making these various claims and accusations, Moscow conveniently ignored the existence of imbalances favoring the USSR in both the conventional and theater nuclear arenas, and rejected out of hand the argument of the United States that the neutron armament is a defensive, anti-tank weapon, intended to offset Soviet conventional superiority in Europe.

Moscow's charges were amplified in Europe through a broad variety of official and unofficial Soviet sources. Brezhnev, for example, personally sent a letter to Western heads of government warning that production and deployment of the neutron weapon would seriously threaten detente. Similar letters from the Supreme Soviet and from Soviet "trade union" officials were dispatched to Western parliamentarians and labor leaders. Soviet commentary in both *Pravda* and *New Times* took a harsher position, asserting that the weapon not only threatened detente but also greatly increased the likelihood of nuclear war in Europe.

In sum, it was argued, the United States was attempting to turn Western Europe into a hostage of American military policy by imposing the neutron weapon on its allies. As an article in *New Times* claimed:[131]

There can be hardly any doubt that the neutron bomb is a weapon intended for use in Western Europe. For where else is there such a concentration of buildings which the neutron strategists are out to spare. The argument advanced in favor of the neutron bomb . . . is that it is a "clean bomb" which will not destroy Western Europe's churches, houses, or factories. . . . The flaw in this argument is that it proceeds from the premise that the Americans are unlikely to use the present nuclear weapons in Europe because of a sentimental reluctance to destroy buildings and other values. . . . That sentimentality is not a Pentagon trait is clear enough from the experience in Vietnam.

The author then went on to argue that the real purpose of the weapon is to make possible the more effective prosecution of war in Europe. The article continued:[132]

The inventors of the neutron bomb boast that it has still another advantage from the standpoint of NATO "forward strategy." It does not contaminate the battlefield with radioactive fall-out to the same extent as a "dirty" bomb. One merely has to clear away the corpses and keep on pressing ahead without interruption. This "advantage represents another downward step in the moral degradation of present day militarism."

Soviet commentary during these months also included increasing emphasis on the growing worldwide opposition to US deployment of the neutron weapon. The Soviets frequently reported on demonstrations, speeches by important individuals, and the formation of opposition committees in Europe, where this sentiment was strongest.[133]

In 1979, a growing propaganda campaign against NATO's plans to modernize its intermediate-range nuclear forces (INF) replaced the campaign against the neutron weapon as the major theme utilized by Moscow in its attempts to misrepresent US military policy and weaken NATO cohesion. The anti-INF campaign now became the central element in the Soviet Union's overall effort to characterize the American stance as militaristic and to encourage the emergent peace movement in Europe. This propaganda thrust proceeded even as the United States and the USSR approached the signing of the SALT II treaty (which took place in Vienna on June 18, 1979).

On December 10, 1978, *Pravda* charged that the "forces of imperialism and reaction have been activated in the US."[134] Even after the SALT II signing, Moscow cautioned that "the Committee on the Present Danger, the American Conservative Union, and the Coalition for Peace Through Strength," all of which were seen as "well paid by the military-industrial complex," were conducting an effective countrywide mass media campaign to prevent US ratification of the treaty.[135] By the late summer of 1979, not only did the Soviets see ratification of the SALT II agreement slipping away, but also felt cause to report that "the hawks campaign had resulted in an increase in the new defense budget, as well as the decision to go forward with the development of new nuclear weapons"—the most important component of which was the decision to modernize NATO's nuclear capabilities.[136]

In December 1979, at a special meeting in Brussels, NATO foreign and defense ministers decided to undertake the modernization of NATO's theater nuclear forces through the production and eventual deployment of 572 Pershing II and cruise missiles. Earlier in the year, as the NATO ministers began the deliberations which would lead eventually to this decision, Moscow responded immediately with an intensive propaganda campaign aimed at developing an environment of public opinion in Western Europe opposed to INF modernization. As in the case of the anti-neutron weapon effort, Moscow's new campaign took a variety of forms. Included were the use of public and diplomatic gestures, overt propaganda, and covert press placements, and the employment of West European Communist parties and international front groups.

To a great extent, the principal themes set forth during the propaganda assault against NATO's modernization plans mirrored those employed during the earlier effort against the neutron weapon. INF modernization would generate an American-caused escalation of the arms race in Europe, it was argued, thereby increasing the likelihood of nuclear war.[137] The Soviet nuclear modernization program does not pose a threat to Western Europe, Moscow asserted, and hence there existed no justification for NATO's decision to upgrade its nuclear forces.[138] As *Pravda* pointed out, the INF decision would impose high financial costs on NATO, and therefore was opposed by many Europeans.[139] Moscow noted further that the NATO decision would force the Soviet Union to strengthen its own nuclear capabilities in response.[140] Finally, *Pravda* claimed the US proposal in reality was intended to function only as a bargaining chip for purposes of blackmailing the Soviets in the SALT negotiations, and was not designed primarily for the defense of America's NATO allies.[141]

As the time for the NATO decision approached, the amount of Soviet propaganda coverage granted to the subject increased, and the tone employed grew harsher. In late October 1979, an article in *New Times* asserted that NATO plans "aimed not simply at modernization," but in fact were designed as a "nuclear bludgeon" to be "used against the USSR in the event of war"—an outcome rendered more likely by the very NATO proposals under consideration.[142] By late November, Moscow was characterizing the NATO deliberations as an American-directed "NATO Missile Frenzy," and—by early December— as a component of "Hegemonist Geopolitical Thinking."[143] After the decision finally was made in December in favor of INF modernization, Moscow continued to warn Europe of the consequences. *New Times* stated:[144]

> Commenting on the Pentagon's plans, the West German magazine *Der Spiegel* writes: "Deployment of nuclear missiles will bring Washington one advantage: it will no longer have to guarantee the defense of Europe and risk having its own territory destroyed in the event of war. In the future, the United States will be able to confine not only ordinary but also nuclear conflict to Europe."

This is highly debatable, but the desire to put others in jeopardy and to remain on the sidelines is obvious.

Opposition to the neutron weapon and to INF modernization constituted the principal propaganda themes utilized by the Soviets during 1977, 1978, and 1979 in their efforts to divide the NATO alliance and encourage the growth of peace movements in the West. However, in addition to these issues, major emphasis also was placed on the theme of US imperialism in the Third World, especially with respect to American interference in the efforts of the Soviet Union to offer aid to developing countries. The central thrust of this commentary appears to have been designed to offset US criticism of Soviet involvement in Africa (and elsewhere in the Third World) by presenting the United States as the opponent of liberation struggles.[145]

Coverage of this theme focused on Angola during the 1976–1977 time segment, shifted to Ethiopia in 1978, and concentrated on Afghanistan in 1979.[146] In addition to these situations, the only other set of circumstances related to US-Third World affairs which received close attention was the upheaval in Iran during the latter part of this period. As might be expected, this "failure of US imperialism" received extensive coverage in Soviet propaganda sources.[147]

An examination of the Ethiopian case serves to illustrate the general approach employed by the Soviets in this subject area. Moscow characterized its intervention in this country as assistance to the "Ethiopian Revolution," which was portrayed as the "victim of aggression" promoted by the United States. In the words of *New Times*, the Soviet Union "at the request of the Ethiopian government . . . renders material and technical assistance," while the United States and its allies had "seized upon the internal struggle in Ethiopia to destabilize the situation in the Horn of Africa."[148]

The Soviets set forth a variety of other minor propaganda themes during the 1976–1979 period which focused either on the United States *per se* or on the US-European alliance (e.g., commentary on the growing social and economic crises afflicting the Western societies). One further component of Moscow's propaganda effort during these years, however, requires special discussion: the Kremlin's major campaign throughout this period against the CIA.[149] Moscow's assault comprised a broad range of charges, too numerous to examine here. Nevertheless, it should be noted that these accusations in general appear to be consistent with the long-term Soviet objective—instituted almost immediately after the inception of the CIA in the late 1940s—of defaming the Agency by portraying it as an arm of American imperialism, assisting only dictatorial regimes and employing the most devious and draconian methods. Two brief examples serve to demonstrate Soviet use of this propaganda approach.

In 1977, *New Times* published a rather lengthy, two-part sequence entitled "On the Trail of a President's Killers." Focusing on the "sinister forces" behind the assassination of President John F. Kennedy, the author of these articles pointed an accusing finger at the CIA and the military-industrial complex. *New Times* stated:[150]

> In the autumn of 1963 President Kennedy ordered an end to the sabotage raids against Cuba. . . . This was met with strong resistance by the intelligence agencies. . . . The President was also considering putting an end to the American military intervention in Indo-China, which angered the Pentagon and prompted it to join forces with intelligence against the White House.

Since it was "impossible to remove Kennedy by legal means . . . the only alternative left for his opponents was to kill him," the author continued.[151] The remainder of the sequence purportedly revealed how these events were covered up, and concluded with the observation that in the United States "political assassination has become an established tradition."[152]

An extensive four-part series appearing in *New Times* in the fall of 1979, under the title "Langley Silhouettes,"[153] provides a second example. This series, which allegedly drew part of its

evidence from US Congressional hearings, presented a history
(beginning with the early 1950s) of activities conducted by the
CIA—"a centre of espionage, provocation, and subversion that
has no parallel to human history."[154] The charges levied against
the CIA in these articles were reflective of the post-World War II
Soviet propaganda effort directed against the US intelligence
community.

New Times now characterized the CIA as "one of the main
tools of the US ruling elite, who would like to remake the world
in a way that would best suit their purpose, to impose every-
where their kind of order."[155] To assist in this goal, the series
continued, "the CIA's job is to conduct psychological warfare,
and 90 percent of its resources go for this purpose." The underlying motivation is nothing short of a desire to "subvert the state
system of the country chosen as the target . . . this is the purpose
for which the Agency was established, its raison d'etre."[156]

LONGITUDINAL ANALYSIS OF
SOVIET PROPAGANDA THEMES

The previous section of this chapter presented a description and
explanation of the results found through a textual analysis of
Soviet foreign propaganda published between 1960 and 1980. In
the present section, Soviet propaganda trends will be examined
quantitatively, through a longitudinal analysis of the commentary appearing in *Pravda*'s "International Review."

On the basis of quantitative content analysis, we have found
it possible to classify Soviet commentary on the United States
and NATO into ten thematic categories (described earlier in this
chapter). The themes have been rank ordered, according to the
relative frequency with which each appeared in "International
Review" during specific periods of time (in this study, measured
in a series of twelve-week units). For example, a score of 100
percent for a particular theme during a given twelve-week period
would mean that all the Western-related issues and events cov-

ered in "International Review" during that time segment were directly associated with only that theme.

Table I presents in summary form the general results of our content analysis of "International Review" for the several two- or three-year spans examined in this chapter. (To be reported in the table, a theme must have received at least 10 percent of the total commentary on the United States and NATO during a particular time span.)

TABLE I. TRENDS IN MAJOR THEMES OF SOVIET PROPAGANDA

	Aggressiveness	Militarism	Threatening Bloc Unity	Crisis in the West	Opposition to Negotiations	Realism
1960–1962	69%*	15%	—	—	—	—
1967–1969	79%	—**	10%	—	—	—
1976–1979	25%	10%	12%	12%	20%	10%

*Figures represent percentage of Western-related commentary appearing in "International Review" received by each theme during a given period.

**Represents score of less than 10 percent.

The results of this quantitative analysis are consistent with the broad trends in Soviet propaganda already identified in our descriptive textual analysis. The quantitative analysis reveals, to begin with, that as the number of issues and events discussed in "International Review" increased during the course of the 1960–1980 period, the number of propaganda themes employed also increased. Assertions of American and NATO aggressiveness constituted the predominant theme during the early 1960s; 69 percent of all commentary on the West was related to this contention. Only one other theme—the closely related issue of militarism—reached or exceeded the 10 percent mark (and hence was included in Table I). These findings directly parallel the descriptive analysis presented for the 1960–1962 period.

During the 1967–1969 time span, Soviet commentary was

even more one-sided, with references to aggressiveness encompassing 79 percent of all opinion expressed on the United States and NATO. This quantitative outcome is not surprising, in view of the extensive coverage devoted by both *Pravda* and *New Times* during these years to the American involvement in Vietnam. As discussed previously, Soviet commentary on the Indochina question took a number of different but interrelated forms, and Moscow undertook a systematic effort to associate this issue with various domestic and international problems faced by the United States. Other issues linked with the aggressiveness theme during this period were the danger of German revanchism and US manipulation of NATO for the purpose of achieving Washington's own expansionist goals. The only other theme receiving at least 10 percent of the coverage during these years was the assertion of Western threats to the unity of the Communist bloc, through subversive efforts and anti-Soviet propaganda. This charge was related specifically to the events surrounding the Czech crisis of 1968.

Six of the ten themes identified in this study achieved a score of at least 10 percent in the quantitative analysis conducted for the 1976–1979 time segment, as indicated in Table I. These findings also corroborate in quantitative terms the conclusions presented in our descriptive analysis. During these years, the negative theme of aggressiveness dropped to 25 percent of the coverage received, while the more positive theme of realism now rose to achieve a score of 10 percent. This should not be taken to mean, however, that a more equitable balance now was achieved between positive and negative commentary—for while coverage of aggressiveness did decline, other negative indicators now received significantly more attention than in previous periods. These increasingly emphasized themes (and their coverage scores) included militarism (10 percent), threatening bloc unity (12 percent), opposition to negotiations (20 percent), and crisis in the West (12 percent). It is clear that Soviet propaganda remained overwhelmingly negative, with 80 percent of all commentary on the United States and NATO comprising negative themes.

Finally, several minor themes also received more coverage

during the 1976–1979 period, although they did not reach the 10 percent mark. For example, the theme of the unreliability of American foreign policy was not apparent during the early 1960s, and the theme of US collusion with other enemies of the USSR did not appear in either the 1960–1962 period or the 1967–1969 time span. During the 1976–1979 period, however, each of these themes appeared more frequently, with American foreign policy unreliability associated with the SALT process and the collusion issue linked to US relations with China. During the two segments of the 1960s examined in this chapter, half of the ten themes identified received less than 2 percent of the Western-related coverage included in "International Review." During the 1976–1979 years, however, only the theme of Western human rights violations averaged less than 2 percent of the coverage presented.

COMPARATIVE LONGITUDINAL ANALYSIS

In the preceding portion of this chapter, Soviet propaganda themes were examined from a quantitative-longitudinal perspective. This approach will be continued in the present section, with an assessment of these themes in a comparative mode and in combination with one another. The following questions will be addressed: What has been the relative weight accorded to negative as opposed to positive commentary about the United States and NATO? To what degree does Moscow view the United States and NATO as a threat? How has Moscow utilized indications of social, economic, and political problems in the West?

Negative Versus Positive Commentary

The descriptive textual analysis of Soviet propaganda during the 1960–1980 period presented earlier showed that while Soviet commentary became somewhat less strident during the

1970s (due to increasing emphasis on so-called Western realism), overall it remained consistently negative. In the next section, this conclusion was confirmed quantitatively. Here our quantitative findings will be displayed graphically. Emphasis will be placed on a comparison of positive commentary concerning realism and the following negative indicators of American and NATO behavior: aggressiveness, hostility (a synthesis that combines the themes of aggressiveness, militarism, and threats to Communist block unity), and opposition to negotiations.

Graph I, which compares realism with aggressiveness, reveals an important difference between the 1960s and the late 1970s. Throughout the 1960s, references to US and NATO aggressiveness—including adventurist and provocative behavior, the increase of international tensions, and exploitation of the developing world—dominated Soviet propaganda. (Between 50 percent and 98 percent of all commentary on the West consisted of such references.) The theme of Western realism, on the other hand, received negligible coverage during the 1960s. During the 1976–1979 time segment, by contrast, aggressiveness declined to between 9 percent and 41 percent of all Western-related coverage in "International Review," while the portion of commentary devoted to Western realism fluctuated between 10 percent and 20 percent.

Thus, while references to realism constituted an average of only 1.6 percent of all commentary devoted to the United States and NATO during the 1960s, the corresponding figure rose to almost 10 percent during the 1976–1979 years. As demonstrated in Graph I, the lowest levels of references to aggressiveness either coincided with or immediately followed the peaks of coverage concerning realism. It also should be noted that the two periods in which realism received the most emphasis were the first year of the Carter presidency and the summer of 1979 (which brought the signing of the SALT II agreements).

While the data presented in Graph I tend to be consistent with our earlier descriptive analysis of the 1960–1980 period, the graph in a sense appears to overstate the case by giving an

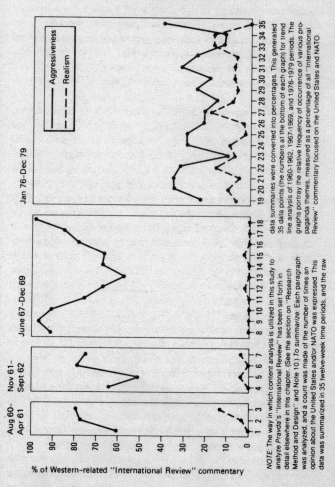

GRAPH I

Themes of (a) *Western Aggressiveness* and (b) *Western "Realism"*

NOTE: The way in which content analysis is utilized in this study to analyze *Pravda*'s "International Review" has been set forth in detail elsewhere in this chapter. (See the section on "Research Method and Design" and Note 10.) To summarize: Each paragraph was analyzed, and a count was made of the number of times an opinion about the United States and/or NATO was expressed. This data was summarized in 35 twelve-week time periods, and the raw data summaries were converted into percentages. This generated 35 data points (the numbers at the bottom of each graph) for trend line analysis of 1960-1962, 1967-1969, and 1976-1979 periods. The graphs portray the relative frequency of occurrence of various propaganda themes, measured as a percentage of all "International Review" commentary focused on the United States and NATO.

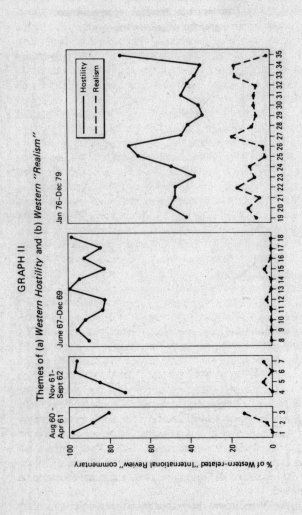

GRAPH II

Themes of (a) Western Hostility and (b) Western "Realism"

impression of greater balance between positive and negative commentary than in fact was the case. Aggressiveness, however, is only one of a number of propaganda themes used by the Soviets to characterize the United States and NATO in negative terms. For this reason, the hostility measure—which combines the themes of aggressiveness, militarism, and Western threats to Communist bloc unity—is a more appropriate indicator with which to compare the theme of Western realism.

As Graph I reveals with respect to aggressiveness, Graph II depicts a decline in negative commentary (i.e., coverage devoted to hostility) in the 1976–1979 time segment as compared with the 1960s. However, the closeness of the association between the rise of positive commentary and the decline of negative commentary is much less apparent than in Graph I. In other words, while the proportion of coverage devoted to realism during the 1976–1979 years averaged nearly 10 percent, the combined hostility measure nevertheless accounted for an average of 50 percent of all Soviet commentary on the West published in "International Review" during this segment. A brief look at the militarism theme will help to explain this difference.

Graph III portrays a significant rise in references during the late 1970s to Western (primarily American) militarism. The trend line depicting the proportions of coverage devoted to this theme jumps from figures averaging 8 percent during late 1976–early 1977 to 25 percent during the following summer and 35 percent in the fall of 1977. This abrupt rise illustrates the growth of Soviet criticism of those forces in the United States which opposed detente and advocated a military buildup. Additionally, it was during these months that the SALT II negotiations broke down and the Carter Administration charged the Soviet government with a number of human rights violations. This upward trend declined with the signing of the SALT II agreements, but began to increase rapidly again in April 1979. By the end of the year, 20 percent of all Western-related commentary focused on militarism.

Graph IV indicates the percentage of Soviet commentary which was devoted to the theme of US refusal to negotiate with the USSR. This theme—although not factored into the hostility

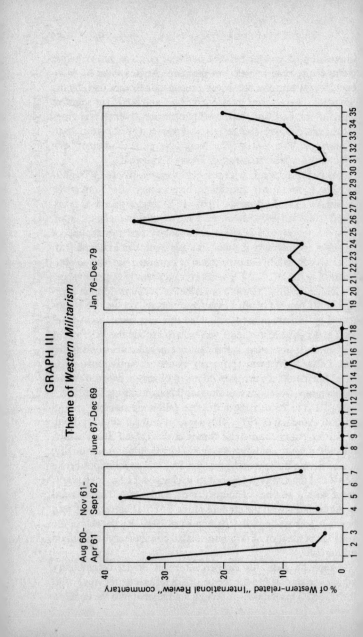

GRAPH III

Theme of *Western Militarism*

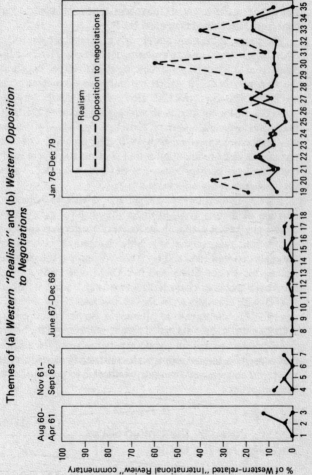

GRAPH IV

Themes of (a) Western "Realism" and (b) Western Opposition
to Negotiations

measure—is another indicator of negative propaganda aimed at discrediting the West. During the 1960s, this theme virtually was ignored; but by the 1976–1979 time segment, it constituted an average of 20 percent of "International Review" commentary concerning the United States and NATO.

The course of the trend line appears to parallel the state of the SALT negotiations underway during this period. Thus, the line drops from a high of 60 percent during 1978 to 10 percent during the first part of 1979, when the talks were completed and agreement had been reached. However, the curve shows an upward turn for the period in which ratification of the treaty became increasingly uncertain, and a figure of almost 40 percent was reached by the summer of 1979. The proportion of commentary devoted to this subject trailed off to 10 percent by the end of the year, perhaps because Soviet leaders decided to stress the harsher theme of militarism.

In sum, a quantitative examination of references to the combination of themes grouped under the hostility measure and commentary associated with the theme of Western opposition to negotiations suggests that very little change took place during the years between 1960 and 1980 in Soviet propaganda directed against the United States and NATO. In other words, while Moscow's negative characterization of the United States and NATO was less intense in the 1970s than in the 1960s, it nevertheless continued to dominate Soviet commentary. Although the Soviets did include some references to the emerging supporters of realism and detente in the West, for the most part Moscow's foreign propaganda consistently carried a negative thrust and remained extremely critical in its portrayal of the Western states.

Threats Posed by the United States and NATO to the USSR

The notion of threat indicates a more direct and immediate danger than does aggressiveness. The latter theme of Soviet propaganda, as defined in this study, refers to adventurism, provocative behavior, actions leading to an increase in international tension, and interference to the politics of Third World nations. Moscow typically utilizes the aggressiveness theme in a rather theoretical manner to characterize the fundamental "nature" of the United States and the NATO alliance. Themes focusing on the idea of threat, on the other hand, suggest a much more immediate danger, and the existence of an actual—rather than a theoretical—challenge.

A closer look at the hostility measure discussed above suggests that two of its constituent themes—militarism and the threat to Communist bloc unity—can be interpreted as signifying an immediate danger. This also appears to be true of the theme focusing on alleged Western collusion with an enemy of the USSR. The propaganda thrust centering on the threat to Communist block unity seems to reflect an immediate and direct challenge, while the other two themes appear to suggest threats which are more long-term in nature.

As shown in Graph V, Moscow's accusation that the West threatened to undermine Communist bloc unity constituted a minor aspect of "International Review" commentary in the early 1960s. In 1968, however, it rose abruptly as a proportion of commentary, and then declined to its former level in 1969. During the 1976–1979 time segment, the proportion of Western-related commentary devoted to this theme fluctuated between 10 percent and 20 percent. After averaging a coverage score of only 3.5 percent during the 1960–1962 years, this propaganda thrust received 43 percent of coverage during August-October 1968, and then declined to a score of zero in 1969.

It is interesting to note the sequence of events that occurred during the period of greatest propaganda attention to this subject. The cause of the rise in coverage appears to have been the crisis in Czechoslovakia, which culminated in the Soviet invasion of August 20, 1968. Charges of a Western threat to bloc unity received greater attention in the months immediately *following* the invasion than in the period immediately *preceding* it. The Kremlin's stress after its troops had crushed the rebellion on the alleged existence of danger from the West seems to suggest

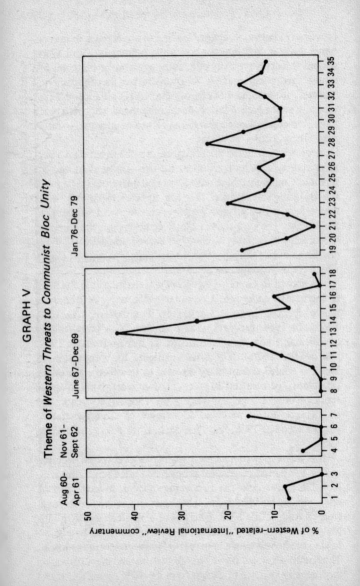

GRAPH V

Theme of Western Threats to Communist Bloc Unity

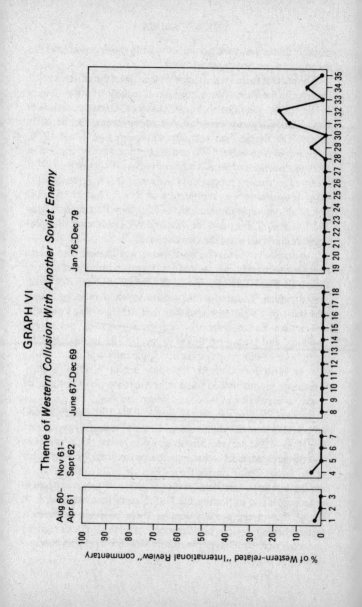

GRAPH VI

Theme of Western Collusion With Another Soviet Enemy

that this theme was used partially to justify the invasion, and did not reflect a genuine sense of threat.

The second theme which appears to suggest the existence of a threat from the West is the accusation of collusion with an enemy of the USSR. (See Graph VI.) Charges of American collusion with West Germany constituted a minor theme in the early 1960s. The theme then virtually disappeared until mid-1978. Begining in November 1978 and continuing through the end of 1979, accusations of Sino-American collusion against the USSR received increasing propaganda attention. This heightened coverage presumably was a reflection of Soviet concern over the potential long-term implications of Zbigniew Brzezinski's May 1978 visit to China, and the January 1979 exchange of diplomatic accords between the two countries.

As noted above, the theme of Western militarism also seems designed to signify the presence of threat to the Soviet Union. Graph III reveals that the use of this theme has been extraordinarily uneven. The abrupt fluctuations appear to reflect the stops and starts of US defense spending and strategic developments, rather than Soviet responsiveness to a genuinely perceived, ongoing, and long-term threat to the USSR. In other words, Soviet use of this propaganda line apparently was not a reflection of Moscow's concern regarding actual Western military power *per se*, but instead was a response to the periodic threat of a serious escalation in Western defense spending.

In sum, despite the clearly predominate anti-American and anti-NATO tone of "International Review" commentary during the 1960–1980 period, careful analysis reveals little evidence that Soviet leaders in actuality perceived a direct Western threat to the Soviet Union during these years. In reality, Soviet use of the three themes connected with the notion of threat appears to reflect an effort to portray the USSR as an innocent victim. It seems that in the employment of these propaganda themes, tactical foreign policy considerations rather than serious security concerns may well have constituted Moscow's primary motivation.

The West in Crisis and NATO Alliance Problems

Moscow's views regarding the inner strengths and weaknesses of Western society undoubtedly contribute to Soviet threat perception, and constitute an important factor in the formulation of the Kremlin's foreign policy and military activities. Two themes covered in "International Review"—crisis in the West and NATO alliance problems—are relevant. The most frequently employed indicators of the West-in-crisis theme are attention to racial divisions, the oppression of the working class, and unemployment of crisis proportions, as well as reiteration of the standard "crisis of capitalism" refrain. Soviet commentary which reflects the theme of problems within the NATO alliance focuses on divisions among the Western allies. In Soviet propaganda, key factors contributing to these divisions are said to include the interference of the United States in West European politics and American pressure on these governments to conform to Washington's preferences.

The coverage of alliance problems—a recurrent theme throughout both the 1960s and the 1970s—fluctuated erratically during the 1960–1980 period, but the proportion of "International Review" commentary devoted to this issue was always relatively low, as indicated in Graph VII. Only twice—in early 1978 and late 1979—did this theme receive as much as 10 percent of all commentary focused on the United States and NATO. These occurrences, which were part of a general trend toward greater coverage of this theme during the 1976–1979 time segment, suggest that Moscow had concluded that the NATO alliance was afflicted with increasing internal tensions. Moscow responded by placing increasing emphasis on "disunity in the alliance" as an important propaganda theme. This assessment coincides closely with our earlier descriptive analysis of the 1976–1979 years.

As the 1960–1980 period proceeded, greater propaganda stress was placed on the theme of domestic crisis within the Western societies. (See Graph VIII.) During the 1967–1969 years, this issue received an important degree of emphasis, with

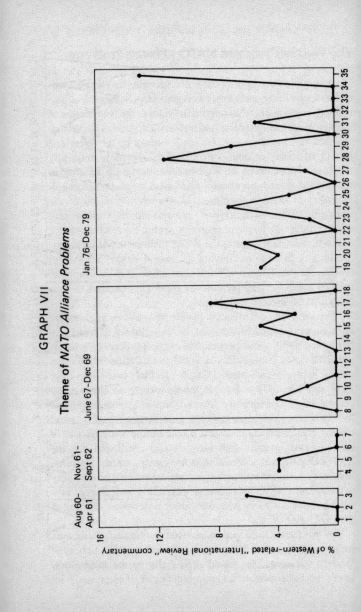

GRAPH VII

Theme of *NATO Alliance Problems*

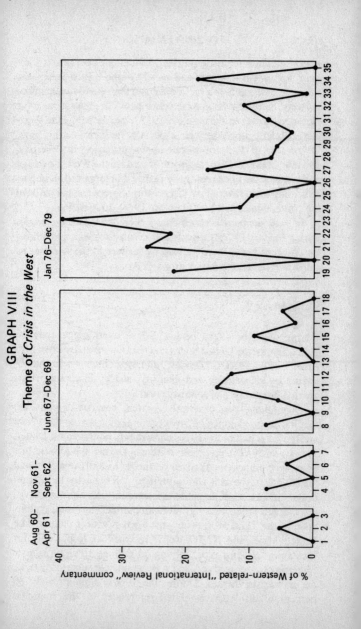

GRAPH VIII

Theme of *Crisis in the West*

% of Western-related "International Review" commentary

Aug 60– Apr 61

Nov 61– Sept 62

June 67–Dec 69

Jan 76–Dec 79

major attention focusing on the debilitating effect of the Vietnam War on the economy and society of the United States, the message of the anti-war movement and the extensiveness of the protests, and race riots in American cities. The greatest coverage occurred, however, during early 1977, when references to Western economic problems were especially frequent. At this time, 40 percent of Western-related commentary in "International Review" was related to the theme of crisis in the West. Coverage of the theme declined rapidly thereafter, but remained an important component (averaging 12 percent) of propaganda related to the United States and NATO for the 1976–1979 period.

In sum, the increasing emphasis accorded these two themes during the late 1970s suggests that divisions within and among the Western states were viewed by leaders in the Kremlin as important targets for Soviet propaganda.

SUMMARY

During the 1960–1980 period, Soviet overt propaganda directed against the United States and NATO—as reflected in both *Pravda*'s "International Review" and *New Times*—was characterized by consistency and intensity, and by increasing complexity, flexibility, and sophistication.

Quantitative and descriptive textual analysis demonstrate that the preponderance of Soviet propaganda during the 1960s and the latter half of the 1970s consistently portrayed the United States and NATO in negative terms. During the 1960s, this negative commentary focused on the themes of American and NATO aggressiveness and militarism. US behavior in international affairs was depicted as adventuristic, provocative, responsible for increasing international tensions, and exploitative of the Third World (i.e., the aggressiveness theme). The United States and NATO were presented as responsible for escalating the arms race, relying on military force to achieve foreign policy objectives, and seeking nuclear superiority (i.e., the militarism theme). During the 1960s, approximately 80 percent of all Western-related references in "International

Review" were associated with these two negative themes—a quantitative finding in accord with the descriptive textual analysis of *New Times* covered in the early sections of this chapter.

During the 1970s, the Soviet portrayal of the United States and NATO generally remained consistent in its negative and defamatory characterization of the West. As was the case in the 1960s, approximately 80 percent of all Western-related propaganda references in "International Review" depicted the United States and NATO in unfavorable terms. However, in addition to the charges of militarism and aggressiveness, other negative themes now were employed. Both the United States and NATO, for example, were said to oppose SALT and any other negotiated settlement of international problems. Moscow accused the United States of interfering in the affairs of the Communist states, and charged that Washington ultimately hoped to subvert Communist bloc unity. In the late 1970s, Moscow also described the West as undergoing a serious economic, political, and social crisis.

These findings are revealing, in light of the fact that the 1970s purportedly were the years of detente and relaxation of East-West tensions. It is important to note that while Soviet propaganda did cover detente and identified the emergence of "realistic" forces in the West, these developments almost always were discussed in terms of the existence of "two contradictory tendencies" in Western behavior. Furthermore, the theme of Western realism received only 10 percent of "International Review" commentary on the West during the 1976–1979 time segment, while the negative themes received approximately 80 percent of all coverage. (Corresponding conclusions were reached in our descriptive textual analysis.) In sum, it is clear that regardless of whether—from the Western vantage point— East-West relations were perceived to be in a period of relaxation (i.e. detente) or intensification of tensions (i.e., cold war), Soviet overt propaganda generally continued to portray the United States and NATO in consistently negative and defamatory terms.

While the United States persistently was characterized as the major threat to world peace, careful analysis of Soviet propaganda indicates that in reality the Kremlin did not perceive any direct threat or challenge to its security interests emanating from alleged US aggressiveness and militarism. The incongruity between Soviet propaganda and Moscow's actual threat perception may be explained partially by considering the tactical foreign policy objectives of the Kremlin—especially the desire to weaken the Western alliance—rather than its immediate security concerns.

Closely related to this characteristic of thematic consistency is the intensity and duration of the messages Soviet foreign propaganda seeks to convey. As has been demonstrated throughout our examination of the 1960–1980 period, general themes such as aggressiveness and militarism are repeated in many and varied forms, virtually *ad infinitum*. Furthermore, the Soviets are able to saturate their media with issues and events related to these themes so as to ensure broad regional or global coverage. Moscow's propaganda campaigns against both the neutron weapon and NATO's INF modernization program provide important examples of this process. Equally revealing was Moscow's orchestration of various propaganda campaigns directed against US involvement in Vietnam.

The growth in the number of issues and events covered during the latter half of the 1970s in comparison with the early 1960s, as well as the degree to which these subjects were combined and interrelated, points to the increasing intricacy and sophistication of Soviet foreign propaganda. As noted above, Moscow's propaganda effort during the 1960s concentrated almost exclusively on one or two themes. By the late 1970s, half a dozen themes were receiving significant coverage. Additionally, the particular events and issues associated with these themes proliferated, demonstrating the growing complexity of Soviet commentary. The range of actors accorded propaganda coverage also greatly increased, so that as much attention was paid during the late 1970s to American subgroups and individuals as to the United States as a whole. By the late 1970s, the Soviets had achieved a quite impressive ability to relate multiple issues and actors to specific themes. Additionally, the language and style of Soviet commentary showed significant improvement as the years progressed. When compared with commentary from the early 1960s, Soviet propaganda published during the late 1970s appears not nearly so dull and ritualistic.

Finally, analysis of Soviet foreign propaganda over the twenty-year period under consideration reveals an increasing flexibility. This enabled Moscow to respond rapidly to critical issues and events of the day. The abrupt emergence of the collusion theme in Soviet commentary as Sino-American relations improved in 1978 is illustrative. The intensive propaganda campaigns launched in immediate response to the US decision to develop the neutron weapon and NATO's decision to modernize its nuclear forces also serve as examples of Soviet flexibility and efficiency.

CHAPTER IV

SOVIET COVERT POLITICAL TECHNIQUES, 1960–1980

THIS CHAPTER EXAMINES the Soviet use of covert (i.e., secret) political techniques to promote and enhance the effectiveness of Moscow's overt propaganda. It will be shown that despite the emphasis on detente, movement toward an arms control agreement, and the presence of other "signs" of relaxation in East-West relations in the latter half of the 1970s, the Soviets continued to expand covert political activities directed against the United States and NATO.

As with overt propaganda, the purpose of secret political action is to persuade, manipulate, mislead, and deceive, and a close relationship exists between the two. The overt propaganda themes directed against the United States and NATO, described earlier, also were advanced through covert channels. Both overt and covert active measures are directly associated with Soviet foreign policy objectives.

Three specific Soviet covert techniques will be described in this chapter. While Soviet leaders engage in a variety of secret operations, here the focus is on international front organizations, agent-of-influence operations, and forgeries.

INTERNATIONAL FRONT ORGANIZATIONS

In an earlier chapter, political warfare was defined as the use of both overt and covert measures, including diplomacy and negotiations, to influence politics and events in foreign countries. The activities undertaken by Soviet-directed international front organizations fall somewhat toward the center of the overt-cover continuum of Soviet political actions. On the one hand, the International Department (ID) of the CPSU's Central Committee coordinates the activities of these organizations. On the other hand, the fronts actively attempt to maintain an image of independence.

The origins of the post-World War II Soviet international front organizations can be traced to the 1920s, when the Communist International (Comintern) organized the first international fronts. Leading Comintern officials assigned an important role to these organizations, which were to function—in effect—as tools of Soviet foreign policy. This was described in the early 1920s by Willi Munzenberg, the Comintern expert on organizing international fronts (which he termed "Innocents Clubs"). In the view of Munzenberg:[1]

> We must penetrate every conceivable milieu, get hold
> of artists and professors, make use of theatres and cin-
> emas, and spread abroad the doctrine that Russia is pre-
> pared to sacrifice everything to keep the world at peace.

In 1922, Karl Radek—a central figure in the Comintern's Executive Committee—spelled out the role which international fronts should play in the early foreign policy of the Soviet state. According to Radek, these organizations were to be employed against Soviet enemies "when we are lacking the necessary strength."[2] In other words, fronts were to serve as an indirect means of conducting an offensive foreign policy against much stronger opponents of the newly established Communist regime. In 1935, Comintern official Otto Kuusinen was more explicit: "We want to attack our class enemies in the rear. . . . But how can we do so if the majority of the working class youth follow not us, but, for instance, the Catholic priests or the liberal chameleons." The answer, according to Kuusinen, was "to create a united youth front."[3]

This commentary by leading officials of the Comintern provides an outline of the initial tasks assigned to front organizations: i.e., these bodies were to employ propaganda and undertake other political measures to promote Soviet foreign policy objectives within the borders of other nations. Judging from the activities of Soviet international fronts during the post-World War II period, it appears that Moscow continues to view these organizations as useful tools for the conduct of political warfare.

Following the conclusion of World War II, responsibility for directing and coordinating the front organizations was assigned to the Communist Information Bureau (Cominform).[4] At its third meeting, in November 1949, the Cominform undertook an initiative leading to a "peace" campaign involving the new postwar fronts. (It should be noted that the initiation of this "peace" effort coincided with the first Soviet atomic test. Hence, at the precise time the Soviets embarked on a campaign to promote the disarmament of the West, they also were engaged in a buildup of their own nuclear forces that continues today.) The essential elements of this thrust were set forth in a report entitled "Defense of Peace and the Fight Against the Warmongers" by Mikhail Suslov, Secretary of the Central Committee of the CPSU (and later, until his death, a member of the Politburo).

Asserted Suslov in his report: "For the first time in history an organized peace front has arisen, which has made its aim to save mankind from another world war, to isolate the warmonger clique, and to ensure peaceful cooperation among nations."[5] He went on to explain that "the peace movement arose as a protest movement of the masses against the Marshall plan and the aggressive Western union and the North Atlantic alliance."[6]

Suslov concluded by observing that "of great significance to the development of the peace movement" are the "Wroclaw Congress of Intellectuals for Peace . . . and especially the World Peace Congress in Paris and Prague . . . at which 600 million organizers for peace were represented."[7]

It was during this latter Congress, which met in April 1949, that the World Peace Council (WPC) was formed. Since its establishment, the WPC has been among the most important and active of the Soviet-directed front organizations. On foreign policy matters, the other fronts appear to follow the lead of the WPC. These organizations include the World Federation of Trade Unions (WFTU), the World Federation of Democratic Youth (WFDY), the International Union of Students (IUS), the Women's International Democratic Federation (WIDF), the Christian Peace Conference (CPC), and several other less active and less broadly-based groups.

The WPC has played a significant role in Soviet efforts to influence political developments in the West over the past thirty years. It is one of the instruments used by the Soviets to reinforce their overt propaganda campaigns. This chapter includes an examination of the activities of the WPC and its interaction with other fronts. Before the major WPC propaganda campaigns are discussed, however, Soviet methods of controlling the WPC will be described. Similar methods apparently are used to control other international fronts.[8]

The Soviet Union and the World Peace Council

Moscow has adopted a low profile in its relations with international fronts. In the years immediately following World War II, the fronts were based in Western Europe. When they were "asked to leave" by Western governments, the fronts moved to neutral countries and to Eastern Europe. Moscow has not sought to have Soviet citizens installed as the presidents and chief administrative officers of these ostensibly non-governmental organizations. Nevertheless, several methods are employed to ensure that the CPSU retains control of the fronts—even though periodically (e.g., after the invasion of Czechoslovakia in 1968) constituent elements are not always as responsive as Moscow might wish.

Moscow exerts its influence in large part by controlling the leaders of both the WPC and its national affiliates. The Presidency, the Secretariat, and the Presidential Committee of the World Peace Council all are dominated by individuals sympathetic—if not completely loyal—to the CPSU. The overwhelming majority of persons in these WPC executive bodies are officials or nationals from the following types of countries and international organizations: the USSR and the East European bloc countries; Communist countries which are outside the Eastern block but loyal to Moscow; Soviet-backed guerrilla movements; non-ruling Communist parties in developed and developing countries that are linked to the CPSU International Department; and other Soviet-controlled international front organizations. Despite occasional difficulties, these officials almost always allow Moscow to have its own way.

The case of Romesh Chandra, the President of the WPC, is a good example. Chandra has been a member of the WPC's Presidential Committee since 1953. He is a long-standing member of the National Committee of the Communist Party of India, one of the foreign Communist parties most loyal to Moscow over the years.[9] For over a quarter of a century, Chandra consistently has promoted Moscow's foreign policy objectives. An article on the recent activities of the WPC which appeared in the ID journal *Problems of Peace and Socialism* (known in its English-language edition as *World Marxist Review*), is illustrative of Chandra's general posture. According to Chandra:[10]

> The activities of the World Peace Council have acquired a new content: 700 million signatures were collected to the WPC's new Stockholm Appeal to Halt the Arms Race and handed over to UN Secretary-General Dr. Kurt Waldheim on the occasion of the Special Session of

the UN General Assembly on Disarmament in May 1978. In Europe, the struggle to curb the arms race has become a mass demonstration against the deployment of new US missiles; in North and Latin America, in Asia and Africa it has developed into mass action against the arms build-up, against the military bases and stepped up tensions in the Indian Ocean, the Persian Gulf, and the Caribbean.

While in Chandra's view these Western defense measures were portrayed as seriously threatening world peace, by contrast the Soviet military buildup was described as contributing to the peace process. "The Soviet Union's military policy," Chandra stated, "fully corresponds to these goals. It is of a purely defensive character."[11]

In addition to Chandra's position as President, the WPC Secretariat and Presidential Committee also are staffed largely by loyal supporters of the Soviet Union, who predominate in each of these bodies.[12] Selected every three years at an international congress of the WPC, the Presidential Committee is the organization's leading executive body. In the late 1970s, the Presidential Committee included 23 Vice Presidents, and representatives from over 100 national peace committees and national and international organizations and movements.

Of the 23 Vice Presidents, three were officials from the USSR, Poland, and East Germany. Three others—from Cuba, Vietnam, and Angola—represented Communist governments loyal to Moscow. Members of two other Soviet front organizations—the WFTU and the WIDF—held Vice Presidential positions. The African National Congress (ANC) of South Africa and the Palestine Liberation Organization (PLO), both Soviet-backed guerrilla movements, were represented. Four Vice Presidential positions were held by non-ruling Communist parties of the United States, France, Argentina, and Italy. Other Vice Presidents included representatives from national-level WPC affiliates in Lebanon, Egypt, and Iraq. As will be discussed below, the leadership of the national affiliates generally (but not always) is dominated by local Communist party members loyal to Moscow.

The composition of the remainder of the Presidential Committee followed the same pattern. Included were three functionaries from the USSR, seventeen from the East European bloc, and six from Communist governments aligned with Moscow (two from South Yemen, and one each from Vietnam, Cuba, North Korea, and Mongolia). Five other members of the Committee were drawn from other international fronts (the CPC, the WFDY, the AAPSO, the IUS, and the WIDF), and three represented Soviet-backed guerrilla movements (the ANC, the Southwest African People's Organization [SWAPO], and the Zimbabwe Patriotic Front). Thirteen members came from nonruling Communist parties connected with the ID, and three represented the generally pro-Soviet governments of Ethiopia, Syria, and Libya. Twenty national-level WPC affiliates also were represented.

The daily business of the WPC is conducted by its twenty-member Secretariat, headed by Chandra. During the latter half of the 1970s, key members of the Secretariat included functionaries from the USSR, Poland, Bulgaria, Hungary, Czechoslovakia, East Germany, and Cuba.[13]

The Soviets appear to employ similar procedures to maintain influence over the national affiliates of the WPC. These national affiliates serve Soviet interests domestically, within their respective states, and support Moscow's positions abroad through attendance at international meetings.

A case in point is the US Peace Council (USPC), founded in 1979. Prior to the formation of this organization, various peace groups associated with the Communist Party of the USA (CPUSA) served as the American affiliate of the WPC. Throughout its history, the CPUSA has been one of the most loyal, pro-Soviet Communist parties in the world. Its leadership receives Soviet directives and funding on a regular basis.[14] Since the late 1970s, the CPUSA has placed high priority on the issues of arms control, disarmament, and the peace movement. Although operating with only a small membership, the organization has initiated letter-writing campaigns, sponsored and participated in demonstrations and rallies, formed coalitions with other organizations, and sponsored seminars and workshops to promote the Soviet position on disarmament and peace and to mobilize the American peace movement.

According to the Federal Bureau of Investigation (FBI), during 1979 the CPUSA established a US chapter of the WPC.[15] This apparently was one component of Moscow's increasing effort to exploit such popular causes as peace and disarmament in the United States. At its founding convention in November 1979, the USPC became an affiliate of the WPC, and the key leadership positions were given to CPUSA members.[16] For instance, the Executive Director of the USPC, elected at the convention, is Michael Myerson. In 1982, the *Party Organizer* —an internal bulletin published by the CPUSA for Party members—identified Myerson as a member of the National Council of the CPUSA.[17]

WPC-related activities in the United States increased noticeably in the late 1970s. According to the FBI, "utilizing various symposia, conferences, demonstrations, and publications, the USPC persistently lobbied for the halt of American nuclear weapons production and deployment, particularly intermediate-range nuclear forces in Western Europe."[18] These observations are borne out by a brief examination of USPC activities since 1979.

Both the USPC and the CPUSA have been actively involved in the nuclear freeze campaign in the United States. They were among the organizers of the campaign's first national strategy conference, held in Washington, DC in March 1981. Among those participating in this initial meeting were Oleg Bogdanov and Yuri Kapralov. Bogdanov, who usually resides in Moscow, is an ID specialist in active measures. Kapralov, also a KGB officer, has participated in a number of nuclear freeze activities in the United States.[19]

Since this initial strategy session, the USPC has taken part in a number of meetings and conferences, at which specific actions have been planned by various peace and disarmament groups. Thus far, the most important effort involved preparations for demonstrations to be held during the UN Special Session on Disarmament in June 1982. According to the FBI, "nearly every instrument of Soviet active measures was directed toward infiltrating and influencing the June 12 Committee, the organization formed to plan and coordinate demonstrations" during the Special Session.[20] The USPC was especially active. One of its leaders, CPUSA official Sandra Pollock, served on the June 12 executive committee.

According to one public account, in addition to Pollock, "four other seats were held by Communists or fellow travelers who officially represented their unions but were backed for admission by the USPC." Furthermore, according to this account, the CPUSA and USPC lobbied hard at executive committee sessions "to tone down the official rally call so that it was not equally addressed to the United States and the Soviet Union."[21] A compromise apparently was reached in the executive committee to focus primarily on American responsibility for the arms race. This was reflected in the official position put forth by the committee prior to the demonstration:[22]

> The demonstration addresses all governments which have developed nuclear arms and which compete in the international arms race, but its primary focus is on the United States government. Possessing more nuclear bombs than all other countries combined and leading the technological, first-strike weapons race, the US government is the least willing to stop its nuclear insanity.

Beyond their involvement in the planning process, the WPC, the USPC, and the CPUSA also were actively involved in the actual June 12 demonstration and other events connected with the UN Special Session on Disarmament. From the registration list of non-governmental organizations at the Special Session, ten other Soviet-sponsored international fronts can be identified as participants. These include the AAPSO, the CPC, the IADL, the IOJ, the IUS, the WIDF, the WFDY, the WFTU, the IIP, and the World Federation of Scientific Workers (WFSW).[23]

Since 1980, the USPC also has sponsored and planned visits to the United States for high-level WPC delegations. These groups have toured major American cities, addressing sizable meetings of academics, students, women, and peace activists. The delegations have stressed the themes of peace, disarmament, and American responsibility for the arms race, and have urged those they addressed to initiate letter-writing campaigns, rallies, and demonstrations.

In addition to providing direction and leadership personnel for the USPC, the CPUSA has been involved in establishing state and local peace committees. In 1980, for example, the Wisconsin Communist Party was instrumental in establishing a Peace Commission which organized local participation and support for USPC activities.[24] Among other objectives, local USPC affiliates seek to mobilize religious leaders, educators, and other public figures to endorse the nuclear freeze.

The WPC maintains ties with national peace committees (of which the USPC is just one example) in more than 130 nations throughout the world.[25] Through local Communist parties, Moscow not only seeks to control and utilize the national Peace Councils, but also to use the latter to control the international organization. When American Communist and WPC leader Myerson travels abroad to WPC meetings, for example, he usually does not deviate from Soviet policy.

Another method utilized by the CPSU to control the WPC, and many of its affiliates, is financial. Moscow provides the bulk of the funds for WPC activities. The available evidence strongly supports this conclusion, although how these arrangements operate is not completely clear.

In spite of the fact that the absence of financial information is used to discredit the organization, the WPC refuses to publish a detailed budget or to explain exactly how it receives its funds. It also refuses to allow any independent audit of its finances. These refusals have been used by the governments of both the United States and Britain to establish in the United Nations that the WPC in fact is funded by the Soviet Union. Indeed, in 1981 the organization was forced to withdraw its application for upgraded non-governmental classification with the Economic and Social Council of the UN (ECOSOC) when Western governments effectively maintained that WPC funds almost certainly were derived from the Soviet government.

The US government has gone even further, releasing its own calculations on WPC expenditures and revenue sources. Both the CIA and former Soviet bloc intelligence officers have maintained that the WPC is funded almost completely by Moscow. In 1980, the CIA calculated that the Soviets were spending $63 million annually in support of thirteen major fronts. The WPC —with a full-time staff of 45 and an annual budget of approximately $30 to $40 million—reportedly absorbed the lion's share of this expenditure.[26]

These general conclusions also are supported by Ruth Tosek, a former interpreter for several international fronts. In 1980, she wrote that based on her experience, "all funds of these organizations, in local and hard currency, are provided above all by the Soviet Union, but also by other East European satellite countries on the basis of set contribution rates, paid by the governments of these countries through various channels."[27]

The evidence, of course, is not conclusive. It does indicate strongly, however, that Moscow and fraternal bloc Communist parties provide the major—if not the total—funding for the WPC.

Just how the Kremlin coordinates personnel and funding to turn the WPC in desired directions also is not clear. However, the major vehicles appear to be the International Department of the CPSU and the KGB. These functions apparently are carried out through: (a) ID personnel who are official WPC leaders (e.g., Deputy ID Chief V. Shaposhnikov) or ID personnel who coordinate front activities without official WPC roles (e.g., Y.F. Kharmalov), as well as Soviet personnel in the WPC Secretariat itself (e.g., I. Belyayev); and (b) ID coordination of the selection and financing of national Communist party leaders who support Soviet positions. The KGB assists by secretly financing and coordinating both national Communist parties and the WPC.[28]

The WPC and the other international fronts have supported, almost unswervingly, Soviet public policy. From their origins in the 1940s through the early 1980s, these organizations almost never have deviated from the official Soviet line.

Early WPC Propaganda Campaigns

A principal purpose of the post-World War II Soviet-sponsored peace and disarmament movement has been opposition to American policy and the North Atlantic alliance. Soviet leaders have made this point repeatedly. Suslov, for example, maintained in 1949 that "the North Atlantic alliance of imperialists under the aegis of the USA represents a threat to all progressive mankind."[29] Turning next to the question of means, Suslov noted that:[30]

> particular attention must be given to bringing into the peace movement trade unions and women's, youth, cooperative, sports, cultural and educational, religious, and other organizations as well as scientists, writers, journalists, cultural workers, members of parliament and other political and public men and women who come forward in defense of peace and against war.

Promotion of the "Stockholm Peace Pledge" was the first major campaign mounted by the WPC. Released in March 1950 by the WPC, the pledge stated:[31]

> We demand the absolute banning of the atom weapon, arm of terror and mass extermination of populations. . . . We consider that any government which would be first to use the atom weapon against any country would be committing a crime against humanity and should be dealt with as a war criminal. . . . We call on all men of good will throughout the world to sign this appeal.

In November 1950, leaders at the Second Congress of the WPC, held in Warsaw, claimed that 500 million people had signed the Stockholm Pledge.[32] The targets against which this effort was directed were the United States and NATO. Throughout the 1950s and the 1960s, the decades during which the United States held a nuclear advantage, "ban the bomb"—i.e., disarmament—was a central theme of Soviet propaganda.

Once the WPC peace and disarmament campaign was underway, other Soviet international fronts followed the lead of this group and organized similar propaganda efforts. During the 1960–1980 period, as will be demonstrated below, coordination of the propaganda themes and the political activities mounted by the WPC and other Soviet front organizations consistently occurred. During the early period of the peace and disarmament movement, the WFDY actively participated in the "Ban the Bomb" signature campaign. According to the July 1950 issue of the WFDY magazine, *World Youth*: "In the Soviet Union, the bulwark of peace, the Stockholm appeal is warmly supported by all the peoples, and millions upon millions of signatures have already been collected."[33] The apparently close association between the WFDY and the Soviet Union was described by Nikolai Mikhailov, a Soviet participant in WFDY activities:[34]

> It was not only the Komsomol [Young Communist League of the USSR] that helped the Soviet activists to organize the World Federation of Democratic Youth. We also got valuable assistance from the Party Central Committee: we were shown a correct approach to the problems of the youth movement. . . .

In addition to the involvement of the WFDY, the Communist-led trade unions organized by the WFTU also participated in the early peace and disarmament movement. According to Suslov:[35]

> The trade union centers affiliated with the WFTU are playing a big part in organizing the supporters of peace. They are the initiators of the national peace movements in many countries and of national peace committees. The

trade unions have taken a leading part in the organization of protest strikes and demonstrations against the aggressive North Atlantic treaty, and in organizing nationwide petitions and other mass measures in defense of peace and the national independence and liberty of peoples.

Suslov also assigned a role to local Communist parties in this initial peace campaign, directing the "Communist and Workers Parties to head the fight for peace of all the mass public associations, and to lend it a purposeful and effective character."[36]

With North Korea's initiation of the Korean War on June 25, 1950, the WPC (along with the other Soviet overt propaganda and covert channels) shifted its focus. From 1950 to 1953, the WPC concentrated on the issue of Korea. One of the major themes utilized by the Communist Chinese and the North Koreans during the war was the charge that the United States was waging germ warfare in Korea. This accusation was made, for example, in a telegram sent on February 25, 1952 by the People's Republic of China to Professor Frederic Joliot-Curie, President of the World Peace Council.[37] Joliot-Curie, a member of the French Communist Party, then organized a worldwide protest campaign, and sent telegrams to American officials censuring the use of germ warfare.

Further, on April 1, 1952, a meeting of the Bureau of the WPC (a WPC executive body) held in Oslo, Norway issued a protest against American use of bacteriological warfare.[38] On May 17, 1952, Dr. Heinrich Brandweiner, President of the Austrian Peace Council (an affiliate of the WPC), released material at a meeting held in Graz, Austria, purporting to prove the involvement of the United States in germ warfare. This material then was published in pamphlet form by the Austrian Peace Council in June 1952. Much of the "evidence" contained therein consisted of claims made by the Chinese and Korean Communists, and "confessions" from American prisoners-of-war in Communist custody.

Assisting the WPC in the dissemination of the germ warfare charges were the WFDY and the IUS. A 1952 issue of the IUS magazine *World Student News* carried as a supplement the report of a "scientific commission" organized by the WPC to promote these allegations.[39] In the publication *World Youth*, the WFDY accused the United States of using science "to wage bacteriological warfare in Korea." The WFDY statement continued: "Their manner of waging war now consists of spreading insects infected with the bacilli of plague, cholera, typhoid, and other diseases among children, women, and the whole civilian population."[40]

With the end of the Korean War, the WPC and the other Soviet front organizations turned their attention once again to the Western alliance. All the major instruments of Soviet foreign propaganda and political influence now were refocused on efforts designed to serve Moscow's major objective of splitting the United States and its NATO allies. In this connection, the activities of the WFTU were closely coordinated with those of the WPC. In 1961, the WFTU General Secretary declared to the Fifth WFTU Congress (held in Moscow) that active opposition to the United States and NATO constituted one of the organization's central responsibilities. He stated:[41]

> It is essential to rouse the masses of the workers and peoples in all countries to act in unison against the policy of strength and the aggressive plans of the imperialists so as to avert the danger of war.
>
> This explains why trade union organizations must use every opportunity to explain the origin of this danger and condemn the aggressive strategy being conducted by American imperialism against the socialist camp.
>
> This strategy is carried out by the setting up of an ever-larger number of imperialist military bases and the activities of imperialist military blocs organized under the North Atlantic Treaty (NATO) and the South East Asia [Treaty Organization] (SEATO), and the Middle East [Treaty Organization] (CENTO). These blocs are directed in the first place against the Soviet Union and the socialist countries, and against the national liberation movements and the independence of the people.

During the decade of the 1960s, the WPC continued to concentrate on opposition to all programs and policies of the United States and NATO. This focus has been authoritatively expressed by Chandra, President of the World Peace Council. Reflecting back on the decade, Chandra asserted in 1971 that "the greatest threat to peace both in Europe and other regions of the world is the US-dominated NATO alliance: Europe is divided into two military blocs." However, he continued, "the fangs of NATO can be felt in Asia and Africa as well . . . the forces of imperialism and exploitation, particularly NATO . . . bear the responsibility for the hunger and poverty of hundreds of millions all over the world."[42]

The other Soviet front organizations followed the position set forth by the WPC. This is borne out, for example, by an examination of the final resolution on the United States and NATO issued by the Eighth Congress of the IUS in 1964. The resolution "requests the governments of the United States, Great Britain, and France immediately to proceed to liquidate their overseas military bases and to recall all troops stationed abroad," and "invites the national unions [that belong to the IUS] to voice their protest against the maintenance of overseas military bases and to manifest their full solidarity with the peoples fighting for the elimination of these bases."[43] (The resolution, it should be noted, fails to mention the presence of Soviet troops or bases in East Europe or elsewhere.) The statement concludes by asserting that "the main enemy of humanity and peace is imperialism, headed by the United States."[44] Materials published by the WFDY, the WFTU, and other fronts during this period reveal that these organizations also adhered to this stance.[45]

The consistency during the 1960s between the propaganda line articulated by the WPC and other front groups, on the one hand, and Soviet overt propaganda, on the other, is readily apparent. In both cases, the Western alliance was characterized as an aggressive military bloc and the major threat to peace, while the forces and activities of the Soviet Union and its Warsaw Pact allies were presented as a purely defensive effort.

The Vietnam War—A Major WPC Campaign

During the latter half of the 1960s and the early 1970s, the World Peace Council concentrated increasingly on the issue of US involvement in Vietnam (as did Soviet overt propaganda). In 1971 Chandra outlined the work being done "against the US war in Indochina" by West European organizations affiliated with the WPC, and explained how these organizations combine the Vietnam issue with matters directly related to West European security. Chandra pointed out:[46]

> These movements are linking their struggle more and more with the problems of their own people, above all with the problems of European security of the ending of aggressive imperialist pacts and bases which affect the economies of their countries and the well-being of their peoples.

As part of its campaign against the United States and in support of North Vietnam, the WPC organized "The Stockholm Conference on Vietnam." Between 1967 and 1972, the Stockholm Conference met on an annual basis. Furthermore, it established working committees to conduct activities during the periods between conference meetings. The objective was to establish an organizational mechanism in Western Europe that could conduct active measures against US policy in Vietnam until the war ended. The meetings of this group generally were attended by representatives of the major Soviet international fronts. At the May 1969 meeting, for example, the World Peace Council was represented by a delegation of six, including Chandra. Members of the WFDY, the IUS, the WFTU, the IADL, and the CPC also were in attendance.

The program of action ordered at this gathering called for "an extension of activity against United States products such as petrol, firms providing goods, arms or services for the war in

Vietnam such as Pan Am, and against other non-American firms supplying and feeding the war." Also recommended was "activity to isolate and subject to continuing protest and criticism representatives of the US government." In addition, it was decided, assistance should be given to "Americans abroad in refusing the draft, in defecting from the US armed forces, for carrying on propaganda within the army and for militant action against the Selective Service System." Such assistance might include "pressure for full political rights and security for defectors and draft resisters in various countries and an appeal to all countries to give political asylum to those who refuse to fight in Vietnam."[47]

The World Peace Council provided guidance and support for the Stockholm Conference on Vietnam. Information Letter #2 of the Stockholm Conference, dated May 7, 1970, reported that the WPC Presidential Committee had unanimously adopted the following resolution the previous day at its meeting in Moscow.[48]

> The latest developments in respect to Indochina make it more imperative than ever before to stop the war of aggression waged by the United States. All organizations, all peoples of the world, who stand for peace, freedom and independence must unite in their effort to demand that the United States stop the war in Vietnam and the whole of Indochina.

In the Letter, it also was declared that:[49]

> The Presidential Committee of the World Peace Council strongly supports the decision for a worldwide mass campaign in favor of the Vietnam Appeal issued by the Stockholm Conference in Vietnam, in combination with the "OUTNOW" project initiated by the US anti-war movement.

Further, the WPC Presidential Committee noted, "there are

immense possibilities in a campaign like this . . . you have the opportunity to develop a campaign on an unprecedented scale."[50]

A World Conference on Vietnam, Laos, and Cambodia organized by the Stockholm Conference was held on November 28–30, 1970. As at earler meetings, most of the international Communist front organizations were represented. Chandra headed the WPC delegation. The Soviet Union also sent a delegation from the "Soviet Peace Fund."

Other components of the WPC campaign against the American involvement in Vietnam could be cited. The examples presented above, however, appear to be representative of the way in which the propaganda and political action campaign of the WPC was correlated closely with the overall Soviet program of overt and covert measures during this period. With the end of the Vietnam War, the fronts again shifted their main focus to NATO. Beginning in the mid-1970s, WPC activities concentrated first on the neutron weapon, and then on the modernization of NATO's nuclear forces.

The WPC Campaign Against the Neutron Weapon

Beginning in 1977, WPC propaganda was directed against the deployment by the United States of neutron warheads in Europe. As was described previously, a major campaign of overt propaganda against the neutron weapon also was carried out by Moscow during 1977 and 1978. (Evidently the great concern shown by the Kremlin leadership derived from the effect that deployment of this specific weapon would have on Warsaw Pact forces in the event of a war on NATO territory.) An examination of the materials used by the WPC in its anti-neutron weapon programs during these years reveals a close resemblance to the approach utilized by Moscow.

During September 1977, for example, the WPC published a pamphlet entitled "Neutron Bombs No!" In the introduction to the pamphlet, written by Chandra, it was argued:[51]

The worldwide campaign launched by the World Peace Council in August 1977 for the prohibition of the neutron bomb is the most powerful mass movement of recent times against weapons of mass destruction and for the ending of the arms race. The call of the World Peace Council has been supported actively by numerous international and national organizations representing literally tens of millions of people in all countries.

Chandra further observed that "in the NATO countries the protest movement has grown," and went on to assert:[52]

. . . in each country actions are especially directed towards demanding that the government concerned declare publicly its opposition to the placing of neutron bombs on its territory and demands that President Carter abandon his perilous policy of stepping up the arms race.

In a World Peace Council Appeal carried in the same pamphlet, the WPC further developed the arguments against deployment of the neutron weapon by labeling the armament a "torture weapon being cynically presented as a so-called 'clean' bomb by the United States administration."[53] The Appeal called for "worldwide actions during the fortnight from October 1–15 *Against the Neutron Bomb and All Other Weapons of Mass Destruction*" (original emphasis), to be carried out by "all national peace committees, peace forces, political parties, and other national, regional, and international movements."[54] The pamphlet also contained statements against the neutron weapon from the WFTU, the CPC, the WIDF, the IUS, and the WFDY.

During 1978, a series of meetings, demonstrations, rallies, and other activities in opposition to the neutron weapon was organized by the WPC in Europe and the United States. From January 25 through January 28, for example, a meeting of the Bureau of the World Peace Council "dedicated to the review of the campaign to 'Ban the Neutron Bomb'" was held in Washington, DC.[55]

On May 22, 1978, the World Peace Council took advantage of the Special Session on Disarmament of the UN General Assembly to present to Secretary General Waldheim what WPC leaders claimed were 700 million signatures in support of disarmament. In an accompanying statement, the WPC strongly criticized the American development of the neutron weapon and the stationing of cruise missiles in Western Europe.[56]

Additionally, on June 3–4, 1978, a meeting of world parliamentarians in New York City organized by the WPC proclaimed support for the Special UN Session. A statement produced by this conference "declared that the production of the neutron bomb accelerates, in a tragic fashion, the arms race," and claimed that "this meeting appeals to parliamentarians and all other elected representatives of the people to reject the fabrication and deployment of the neutron bomb."[57]

To coincide with these activities, the WPC newsletter *Peace Courier* carried numerous reports on the growing protest against the neutron weapon. Material presented in this newsletter closely paralleled reports found in such instruments of Soviet propaganda as *New Times*, *Pravda*, and Radio Moscow. A collection of articles from the *Peace Courier* then apparently was translated and reprinted for use in agitating against the neutron weapon in West Germany. A careful examination of the documentation is required before it becomes apparent that most of the material in this collection originated from international front sources.[58]

Although the West German government had agreed to deploy neutron warheads, President Carter decided in April 1978 to cancel deployment. With this decision, the WPC campaign against the weapon came to an immediate halt. When President Reagan took office in January 1981, however, the possibility of deployment reemerged. In early August 1981, articles began appearing in the American press stating that President Reagan had decided to continue development and production of the weapon. Soviet channels of overt propaganda also chimed in. Almost immediately the charges and slogans which had characterized the 1977–1978 campaign began to reappear. An August 11, 1981 article in *Pravda* charged:[59]

the horrendous decision to produce the neutron weapon is the latest step in the present US administration's adventuristic policies, for the neutron bomb is one of the most refined and barbaric means of mass destruction. It is a weapon which produces an exceptionally high level of radiation, directed not against military targets or hardware but against human beings.

On August 13, 1981, TASS political observer Gennady Shishkin (in a TASS English-language transmission) asserted that "the ruling circles of the United States are in the grips of dangerous insanity. This is the only way to assess President Reagan's decision on the production of neutron weapons and the motives by which he is guided." Shishkin also referred to the decision to develop the neutron weapon as "a cannibalistic philosophy."[60] The "cannibal" slogan was repeated the next day by Soviet journalist Oleg Anichkin over Radio Moscow's Domestic Service. Anichkin charged:[61]

This form of weapon is intended purely for killing personnel, i.e., for killing both civilians and military since it has only a radiation effect. This is why these weapons are so monstrous and cannibal-like. Houses, various structures, military equipment, will remain unscathed. Only people will be killed. They will die either at once or slowly and very agonizingly.

Similarly, the international front organizations almost immediately undertook a replay of the charges they had utilized during the 1977–1978 campaign. For example, as reported in TASS, the WFTU in August 1981 "sharply condemned the cynical decision by US President Reagan . . . as an act of hostility towards working people. . . . This attempt of the US administration to incite a new round of the arms race comes . . . when the Soviet Union . . . put forward concrete and constructive proposals in the interest of . . . removal of the danger of a world nuclear war."[62]

The WPC also brought its forces into play in support of the

The WFDY "fact book" in many respects parallels a WPC booklet entitled *The Global Military Buildup* (also published in 1982), and hence serves to illustrate how closely the propaganda of the WFDY mirrors that of the WPC.

In addition to promoting the Soviet position concerning West European defense policy, the WPC also provides support for other Soviet foreign policy objectives. For example, the Soviet Union supports the PLO, and so does the WPC. The PLO in fact is officially represented in the Council, and provided a member to the WPC delegation which met in Geneva with UN Secretary General Waldheim in 1975.[68] In 1979 the WPC held an international conference to promote solidarity with the Palestinian people, and a central theme of the meeting focused on support for the PLO. As Chandra remarked at the conference:[69]

> Our conference not only extends its total and unconditional solidarity with the Palestine Liberation Organization; it also extends full support to the unity of the Arab governments and peoples who oppose the Pax Americana and the treachery which accompanies it and who are carrying forward the great cause of the Palestinian people.

Finally, when Soviet actions become the target of international criticism, the World Peace Conference may take steps to defend Moscow. For example, when the United States in 1980 and 1981 began to charge the Soviet Union with supporting international terrorism, the WPC convened a meeting of the Presidential Committee which met in Havana in April 1981, apparently to counter these accusations. Commenting on the deliberations of this gathering, Havana radio reported:[70]

> Within the framework of the WPC presidency meeting being held at Havana's Palace of Conventions, WPC President Romesh Chandra held a press conference during which he stated that the terrorists who place in jeopardy world peace are those who produce arms and promote the arms race, concretely the United States and

its NATO allies. Chandra added that the statements by Leonid Brezhnev during the 26th CPSU Congress are sound and translate into the demand by world public opinion favoring peace.

AGENTS OF INFLUENCE

Of the various means employed by Moscow for conducting secret operations in support of foreign policy objectives, the agent of influence may be the most complex and difficult to document. In fact, even skilled counterintelligence officers find it very difficult to follow and unravel orchestrated agent-of-influence operations. As noted earlier, there are several different types of influence agents, including the unwitting but manipulated individual, the "trusted contact," and the controlled covert agent.

The agent of influence may be a journalist, a government official, a labor leader, an academic, an opinion leader, an artist, or involved in one of a number of other professions. The main objective of an influence operation is the use of the agent's position—be it in government, politics, labor, journalism, or some other field—to support and promote political conditions desired by the sponsoring foreign power.

Moscow utilizes agents of influence as one element of a carefully orchestrated effort. Insiders label this orchestration "*kombinatsia*." This refers to the skill of relating, linking, and combining various agents of influence (at various times and in various places) with special operational undertakings, in such a way as to enhance effectiveness. These actions comprise one more component of the joint overt-covert approach employed by the Kremlin.

The KGB generally is responsible for conducting these activities. The first phase entails the development of strong covert personal relationships with important figures in foreign societies. Once such a relationship has been established, the next step is to secure the active collaboration of the individual on matters of mutual interest. In return, the KGB will provide remunerations tailored to meet the specific needs or vulnerabilities of the person involved. In some cases, the form of compensation may simply involve money. However, for the individual who has achieved prominence, the rewards for serving as an agent of influence are more likely to entail assistance in the achievement of political or personal goals.

The Case of Pierre-Charles Pathe

One interesting recent case is that of Pierre-Charles Pathe.[71] Because Pathe was prominent, operated over a long period of time, wrote a great deal, and was caught and tried, it is possible to trace many of his activities. (Interviews also were conducted in France with journalists and former French intelligence officials knowledgeable about Pathe and his 1979 trial and conviction.)

Pathe apparently came to Soviet attention when he wrote an article in 1959 praising the Soviet Union in glowing terms. An invitation from the Soviet ambassador in Paris then led to a relationship between Pathe and the first of several KGB officers with whom he would collaborate. Although Pathe was asked to provide information on French politics and politicians, his major role was as an agent of influence in the media.

In 1961 Pathe began to publish—with Soviet encouragement—a confidential journal entitled *Center for Scientific, Economic, and Political Information*, and started to receive some financial support from Moscow at that time. In addition to producing his own journal, Pathe also wrote for a variety of other French mass media publications under the pseudonym "Charles Morand."[72] It appears that the Soviets did not give completed articles to Pathe for publication; rather, he was provided with general instructions and thematic guidelines upon which to base his articles.

This sort of arrangement is not unusual, as will be discussed in the interviews in Chapter V with former Soviet bloc intelligence officers who handled agents such as Pathe. The relationship between a Soviet case officer and an agent of influence apparently is flexible and based on shared interests, especially when the agent is a prominent individual. Particularly in the latter case, the KGB provides general instructions rather than specific orders.

In 1976 Pathe launched a new biweekly newsletter entitled *Synthesis*, for which he received partial funding from the Soviets.[73] The newsletter focused on French, European, and international political, economic, military, and scientific issues. At its heights, *Synthesis* included among its subscribers 139 Senators, 299 Deputies, 41 journalists, 14 ambassadors, and—interestingly—only 7 private individuals, for a total subscription of 500 in France. Through his newsletter, Pathe hence was reaching 70 percent of the Chamber of Deputies and 47 percent of the Senate. It of course is difficult to assess the degree of influence that *Synthesis* actually achieved.

In 1978 a young member of the French Parliament reported to French counterintelligence officers that he was being courted by a Soviet official, Igor Kuznetsov. The French intelligence community began to conduct surveillance on Kuznetsov. Despite his defensive efforts, eventually Kuznetsov inadvertently led French officials to his clandestine meetings with Pathe. The pair were arrested while passing money and documents. Pathe was publicly tried and convicted of espionage against the state. He admitted to participation in clandestine meetings with the KGB, receipt of small sums of money for articles written on Moscow's behalf, and provision of political analysis to the Soviets. Pathe was sentenced to five years in prison.

In addition to his journals and the articles he published under a pseudonym, Pathe also had a personal role. According to the French news magazine *Paris Match*, Pathe—while not famous—did come to enjoy a certain reputation among journalists, who appreciated his drive and spirit, his analytical ability and clarity of thought, and his ability to write.[74] As the son of a French film pioneer, and the brother-in-law of a Minister, a French Ambassador to the United States, and the president of the state-owned

Renault automotive firm, he was a Parisian insider. He knew people in public life across the political spectrum from de Gaulle to Mitterand. Furthermore, Pathe was in a favorable position to identify for the KGB journalists and politicians whom he judged recruitable, and he may have provided this assistance.

For almost two decades, Pathe served as a Soviet asset whose journalistic influence was reinforced by his personal contacts with figures in high places. It is important to keep in mind, however, that Soviet political operations involve a number of elements—both overt and covert, official and unofficial— aimed, in combination, at target individuals and groups. Pathe was not alone; rather, he should be regarded as one of a number of forces targeted at French leaders.

Pathe produced both covert propaganda and written disinformation on behalf of the Soviet Union. The Moscow-inspired articles which appeared in French mass media publications seem to fall within the category of covert propaganda. The newsletter *Synthesis* falls into the categories of both covert propaganda and disinformation. The targets of *Synthesis* did not comprise a mass audience, but were composed primarily of French journalists and the French political elite. The publication was selective and discriminating in manner, seeking to subtly mislead this elite audience.

Themes Appearing in *Synthesis*

This section analyzes almost all of the seventy issues of *Synthesis* published during its existence from 1976 to 1979. While it is difficult to know exactly which items the Soviets promoted, our assessment of *Synthesis* reveals two general categories of propaganda and disinformation: the denigration of, and attacks on, Western interests and policies; and the defense of the USSR and its allies. Pathe's effort apparently was designed to omit from the publication any material which might render the USSR and its friends vulnerable to criticism, to mute that criticism which could not be avoided, and to include material which actively supported or defended the views of the Soviet Union and/or its allies.

Criticism of Western Interests and Policies

The subject matter of *Synthesis* directed against Western interests and policies can be divided into four basic themes. This overall pattern emerges quite clearly, and is very similar to patterns that are found both in the other examples of covert activity described in this chapter and in the content of overt propaganda analyzed earlier in this book. The four anti-Western themes include fostering mistrust among the NATO allies and their friends, denigrating Western weaponry and defense policies, criticizing French policy vis-à-vis American and NATO political and defense arrangements, and expressing distrust of and censuring the United States. (These themes are not presented in rank order according to their relative importance; all may have been equally consequential, and the four were closely integrated and often combined with one another.)

Fostering Western Disunity. Many articles in *Synthesis* were aimed at the creation of fiction and distrust among the Western allies, with the underlying objective of weakening NATO. The publication thus fits directly into one of the major international political campaigns carried out by the Kremlin in the post-World War II period.

Pathe concentrated much attention in this regard on West Germany—a neighbor to France, and an obvious target. Suspicions that Nazi war criminals had survived to occupy positions in the West German government were raised. An April 1977 issue charged, for example, that "descendants of Hitler sleep in the Germany of today."[75] German measures against terrorism were characterized as repressive, and terrorism itself was portrayed as a sign of profound social crises in West Germany and as evidence of the excesses of the German character. West Germany was described as a state paralyzed by its complexes and by the presence of East Germany, which was depicted as a starkly contrasting model of order and stability.[76] Also conjured up were fears of a nuclear Germany, German economic domination, and special German-American ties.[77]

Many of these charges, it is interesting to recall, appeared frequently in the various outlets of Soviet overt propaganda during the 1960s. However, by the late 1970s—as noted in the previous chapter—Moscow was portraying the Federal Republic in very different terms: it now was depicted as one of the principal forces of Western "realism," and a main proponent of detente. It nevertheless appears that in the Soviet view, anti-German sentiment continued to run high in France, and Moscow apparently believed that promotion of the Nazi theme remained a useful tool in preventing closer relations between Paris and Bonn.

With respect to employing NATO as a target of direct attack, Pathe and his sponsors seem to have exercised caution, for there appeared only one article in which the continuing utility of and need for NATO was forcefully rejected.[78] The offensive mounted by *Synthesis* against any closer French relationship with NATO must be regarded, however, as an attack against the latter (see below). Moreover, the epithet—"Atlanticist"— thrown by Pathe at President Valery Giscard d'Estaing was both anti-NATO and anti-American in intent.[79] This indirect attack against the Western alliance also was carried out through articles stressing the lack of common interest and solidarity between France and NATO. The Western heads of state who participated in the London Summit of 1977, with the exception of those from the United States and France, were depicted as having renounced any foreign policy of their own.

In a May 1977 article, France was pictured as the particular target of an "underhanded" American economic war, and West Germany was dubbed "the milk cow of American suzerainty." US deficits in the balance of payments, the article asserted, allow Washington to "suck the substance" of other states. Europe should cease making unnecessary concessions to the United

States, *Synthesis* continued, and should deal with Washington on a strictly give-and-take basis in economic matters. The article concluded by charging that for years the United States has exploited its European allies (West Germany more than the others), and that Europe has served as a US economic protectorate.[80]

A February 1979 issue of the newsletter argued that Britain's special relationship with the United States had brought London no good, and—on the contrary—had benefited only Washington. Britain's international standing, it was charged, had been reduced to that of a political and financial satellite of the United States. Additionally, the American-Italian plan for cooperation on arms production and sales was described as a poor model to follow, since it was not an agreement between equals.[81]

This basic line of criticism never varied in its general parameters, and *Synthesis* carried no articles acknowledging the existence of common interests between France and the United States, or—more broadly—between Europe and the United States. (It goes without saying that no mention was made of a shared interest among these countries in facing the Soviet challenge.) By contrast, as will be demonstrated below, Pathe appeared to exclude or downplay any differences between the West European states, on the one hand, and the Soviet Union and its friends, on the other. This point is made here to emphasize a key fact: not only should what actually appears in *Synthesis* often be regarded as a form of disinformation, but also what does not.

Western Arms and Defense Policy. Articles also appeared frequently in *Synthesis* which focused on criticism directed at Western defense policy—a thrust closely associated with the theme of fostering Western disunity. The treatment accorded both of these themes in *Synthesis* paralleled and reflected commentary which appeared in the channels of Soviet overt propaganda, as well as the propaganda efforts and political actions carried out by the WPC and other international front organizations. This apparently close coordination among measures executed through various overt and covert channels is revealing, and serves as an indication of the way in which all means deemed effective are utilized in Moscow's international political campaigns and operations.

Synthesis carried a number of articles raising questions— some fundamental—about the necessity of Western defense policies and new Western armaments. (It should be noted that at no time did a similar treatment of Soviet military developments appear, to put the issue into perspective; rather, as will be demonstrated below, the publisher of the newsletter engaged in a consistent effort to downplay Soviet defense questions.) In the single article devoted exclusively to NATO, for example, Pathe asserted that many French politicians were of the view that NATO no longer served any purpose and should be dissolved.[82]

Doubts frequently were raised about the willingness of the United States to defend Western Europe, given the risk of a nuclear attack on the American homeland. In a January 1979 issue, Pathe made the argument that American and Soviet leaders would employ nuclear weapons only if their own territories were directly attacked.[83] In an article on the French nuclear force, Pathe argued that the key to the credibility of this force resides in the fact that it exists solely for the defense of France itself; hence, he continued, a conventional Soviet attack would risk nuclear war only if it were to extend beyond Germany and penetrate into France.[84]

Other issues contained descriptions of the neutron weapon as an inhumane and useless armament, adding nothing constructive to the existing NATO arsenal. The United States was portrayed as having unleashed a major propaganda effort to convince the West Europeans that the neutron weapon in fact is a conventional weapon, and that the use of the armament would not entail stepping over the nuclear threshold. However, Pathe asserted, even the West Germans—whom the Americans were attempting to reassure with this weapon—now had come to understand its real meaning.[85] In an article published in March 1978, Pathe expressed surprise at the fact that several NATO countries were enthusiastic about the cruise missile. This mis-

sile, he charged, would change none of the conditions in a
nuclear war, and did nothing to reinforce the defense of those
countries which already had nuclear missiles.[86]

Two factors should be kept in mind during an analysis of the
material on Western defense arrangements which appeared in
Synthesis. First, at no time did Pathe mention the large Soviet
missile deployments and other aspects of the significant
strengthening of Soviet military power underway during this
period. Second, it should be noted that the withdrawal of France
from the military wing of NATO in 1966 constituted a great
strategic benefit to the Soviet Union and a serious loss to NATO.
The degree to which Soviet active measures played a role in
de Gaulle's decision has never been analyzed. What Pathe (an
active Soviet agent of influence at the time) and others were
writing and saying during the period preceding French military
withdrawal from NATO might provide clues to additional Soviet
channels of disinformation operating at that time. Understanding Pathe's efforts is facilitated by bearing in mind the strategic
results of France's partial disengagement from the Western
alliance.

French Relations With the West. A central focus of Pathe's
work, through the vehicle of *Synthesis*, concerned the positions
taken by France on European defense matters and on Western
cohesion and cooperation. *Synthesis* carried a number of articles
peppering the administration of President Giscard d'Estaing
with attacks and warnings regarding these matters. Emphasis
was placed on developments which might, in Pathe's view,
weaken the independence of French policies or suggest a move
toward rapprochement with the United States and NATO. It
should be noted that while serving as a Soviet agent, Pathe
actively participated in the Gaullist Movement for the Independence of Europe, which he helped to organize.

Early in the life of the newsletter, articles appeared in
Synthesis criticizing the French government for alleged subser-
vience to the United States and accusing Giscard d'Estaing of
being an "Atlanticist." The French President was scolded for

joining others at the London Summit of 1977 in renouncing any foreign policy other than that of the United States. Pathe also made the argument that a Soviet invasion of West Germany would not result in a nuclear war, because the United States would not sacrifice its own cities to nuclear destruction in order to defend the Federal Republic. He further alleged that the belief held by de Gaulle that Western Europe cannot depend on the American nuclear umbrella was becoming more widely accepted.[87]

Another issue of *Synthesis* criticized the intervention of France in Chad, the Sahara, and Zaire as serving no French interests, but only those of other Western states. It was alleged that the West is interested only in the raw materials of Africa. Readers were instructed that no great issues divide France and the USSR; neither, it was asserted, does any true political rivalry exist between these states, since they are not powers of the same order. Pathe also declared that the extended nuclear deterrence policy of Giscard d'Estaing—which called for the possible use of nuclear weapons in circumstances other than a direct threat to French territory—was not credible to the Soviets, and was designed only to reassure the West Germans.[88] (This commentary constituted one variation of a theme often utilized by Pathe —i.e., the assertion that a Soviet advance into West Germany would not set off a nuclear war.)

In an April 1979 article, Pathe argued that American cruise missiles would in no way enhance the defense of such countries as France, which already possessed a powerful arsenal of missiles. French industry and the French government, Pathe warned, should stay away from joint arms production agreements with the United States, since such arrangements might serve to weaken a strong and independent French industrial system.[89]

The American Target. Since World War II, Moscow has regarded the United States as its main opponent and the principal obstacle to the achievement of Soviet policy objectives. It therefore is not surprising that an important part of Pathe's work (in conjunction with other overt and covert activities) focused on portraying the United States as the major cause of international instability and the primary threat to world peace. This anti-American thrust has been evident in the themes contained in *Synthesis* already examined in this chapter. Additional articles appeared in the newsletter, however, which treated various events and policies concerning the United States in an even more direct manner, comprising some of the least subtle of Pathe's writings (and presumably reflecting the attitudes of his Soviet sponsors). The principal themes utilized by Pathe in this effort are outlined (not necessarily in the order of their importance) in the paragraphs which follow.

First, Pathe contributed to the major Soviet propaganda campaign directed against the CIA from 1976 to 1979. American intelligence and security services were portrayed in *Synthesis* as having no redeeming features. Two of the major objectives of a June 1977 article on the assassination of President Kennedy were (a) to create the impression that ultimate power in the United States lies in the hands of the director of the FBI, and (b) to expound the view that the killing of the President could not have occurred without the knowledge of the FBI head, since the latter wished to have the President out of the way.[90]

In another issue, Pathe charged the American intelligence services with helping the former Iranian Prime Minister escape from Iran, and with attempting to create disorder in Khomeini's Iran. Additionally, Pathe asserted, secret clauses involving the CIA were contained in the Camp David agreement between Israel and Egypt. Pathe further asserted that one reason why the United States needs a favorable balance of payments is to pay for its intelligence activities abroad.[91] For the most part, *Synthesis* concentrated only on certain alleged US intelligence activities, rather than replaying the unfavorable publicity regarding American intelligence which was generated by investigations in the United States. (This latter material was used in Soviet overt propaganda, as noted in the previous chapter.)

Another subject emphasized by Pathe was American economic policy and the existence of a fundamental conflict of economic interests between the United States and the West

European countries. This rivalry was projected by Pathe in various ways. The issue of US restrictions on landing rights for the Concorde in the United States was presented as representative of American efforts to maintain a quasi-monopoly of the airlines industry and to hurt its sales in other countries.[92] The United States was said to oppose free trade more than any other member of the General Agreement on Trade and Tariffs (GATT), and was accused of doing everything possible to keep the Common Market impotent.[93] Additionally, Pathe stated categorically, there is no natural need for European trade with the United States. By contrast, he asserted, European and Soviet economic interests are complementary, rather than competitive.

Pathe's targets also included the policies of the United States outside of Europe. Singled out for special emphasis was Latin America; and a number of articles in *Synthesis* were critical of US policies in this region, raising doubts about American motives and purposes. It is worthwhile to note that Pathe in a March 1978 article ignored the question of Cuba's totalitarian form of government and any negative lessons to be derived from the Cuban experiment. Castro's totalitarian rule was accepted as necessary, in part, to destroy the former army and security organizations as a means of forestalling anticipated American attempts to overthrow his government.[94]

In the same article, the rest of Latin America was characterized as being under the influence of the United States, with most government administrations, police forces, and armies totally subordinated to the American "special services." The United States exerts the power of a "colonizer" over the region, it was argued; and the armies of Latin American countries were described as praetorian guards and the true guarantors of American suzerainty. Additionally, a highly critical and polemical account of American intelligence activities in Latin America written by Philip Agee, a former CIA officer, was recommended as an authoritative source on these matters.[95]

With respect to US actions regarding the Middle East, Pathe labeled the Camp David agreement between Israel and Egypt as a "non-conference."[96] In an April 1977 article, American policies toward Iran during the rule of the Shah were portrayed as profiting the West, at the expense of the Iranian people; and Iran was described as a country with an "American" king. The language used by Pathe to describe US policy around the globe occasionally was quite strong and even extreme. Pathe claimed, for example, that "the American empire for thirty years was constructed by force and corruption."[97]

American institutions presented an additional target for Pathe, and questions were raised in *Synthesis* about the democratic credentials of the United States. According to a June 1977 issue of the newsletter, the American democracy has evolved into a "police democracy"—though admittedly not one resembling that imposed earlier by the Soviet "NKVD."[98] (The use of the term "NKVD" may signify reference to the Stalinist era, and an effort to distinguish between that period and the present.)

Inevitably, *Synthesis* carried commentary on America's black racial problem. In another article in this same issue, Pathe reiterated the claim that major organizations in the United States continue to reject any participation by blacks. Killing is an American political method for dealing with the country's black population, it was charged, and the assassination of President Kennedy was depicted as representing an "essential aspect of American democracy." The article also made derogatory assertions concerning the American press, the White House, the FBI, the Warren Commission, and other aspects of American society.[99]

A September 1976 article claiming that US leaders had shown little concern for human rights in countries "they controlled" for thirty years was used to question the sincerity of the United States in the human rights area. Additionally, the American press was accused of following the official government line regarding other US sins of omission and commission.[100]

Defending Soviet Policy and Objectives

The second broad theme evident in *Synthesis*—support for and defense of the policies, practices, and institutions of the

Soviet Union and its allies—can be divided into two major categories. The first is active advocacy, as opposed to silence, on subjects of critical importance to the Kremlin. As noted earlier in this chapter, downplaying matters and issues which adversely affect the USSR, or adopting a position of deliberate silence regarding these topics, are techniques frequently employed by Pathe. These practices are not confined to those matters in which the USSR is directly involved. One should note, in this regard, the way in which Egyptian President Anwar Sadat's peace initiative to Israel was handled in *Synthesis*. However, active advocacy signifies a higher degree of issue importance. The second major category encompasses attacks against those persons, groups, and states which compete with the USSR or are considered an ideological threat.

When these two categories are considered, the sponsorship and purposes of *Synthesis* come into clear focus—and the publication is revealed to be more than the product of an eccentric, anti-American Gaullist. The strident tone of some of the articles related to this second broad theme betrays a commitment to a point of view that might raise suspicions regarding their actual authorship, even if one were not aware of Pathe's status as a Soviet agent. This stridency also results in the loss of any subtlety of approach.

Supporting Moscow. Synthesis supported and defended the Soviet Union and its friends in a number of articles. In a June 1978 issue, the nuclear threat posed by the USSR was downgraded, and Pathe asserted that Moscow would never use nuclear weapons unless Soviet territory were attacked. Pathe's denial of any rivalry between France and the Soviet Union was noted earlier in this chapter. American fears of Communism in Italy and France are unfounded, Pathe also argued, in light of its record in the trade unions and local governments of these counries. Pathe went on to claim that the Soviet Union interferes only in areas "already destabilized" by others, and becomes involved without sending troops; in other words, he asserted, the USSR does not destabilize.[101]

In Pathe's view, for example, Soviet and Cuban involvement in Angola came after the interference of the CIA. Additional arguments made by Pathe included assertions that the Western states—and not the Soviets—were in Africa to acquire raw materials; that leaders in Peking deliberately created differences with the USSR as an outlet for internal discontent; that trouble in Yugoslavia would begin only as the result of a Western-supported Croatian independence movement; and that Western colonial criteria were not applicable to Soviet Central Asia.[102]

Pathe defended Moscow in a number of other situations in which Soviet and Western interests clashed. The argument was made that the Soviet Union had never intended to devote resources to a space effort, and that the United States was responsible for the militarization of outer space. Pathe further charged that the Soviet nuclear-powered satellite which fell from space into Canadian territory may have been intercepted by US killer satellites.[103] It also was claimed that charges of Soviet and East European infiltration of de Gaulle's entourage and of the French intelligence service (the SDECE) were American-inspired.[104] The articles on the satellite and on the charges of infiltration carried the earmarks of an attempt to stem the criticism leveled against the USSR in the aftermath of these events.

Similarly, friends and allies of the Soviet Union were solicitously supported and praised, and their positions were justified, in the pages of *Synthesis*. Pathe defended Vietnam, for example, by arguing that the boat people fleeing Indochina in fact were middle class, and that the ongoing problems in Indochina stemmed from previous American actions. China's 1979 attack on Vietnam was called unsupportable, and pro-Soviet Vietnam was praised.[105] Another Soviet ally, East Germany, was singled out for special commendation. This contrasted with Pathe's treatment of West Germany. East Germany was described as stable, afflicted with few problems, enjoying economic progress, and in a position to teach Western Europe some lessons. East Germans were said to regard the Berlin Wall as a defense against infiltration "by American imperialists and their satellites in Bonn." Likewise, the repression of Cuba under Castro was depicted as necessary for the defense of that country against American intelligence activities.[106]

With respect to events in Cambodia, *Synthesis* undertook a flagrant shift in position to conform with Moscow's line. A September 1977 article expressed reservations about charges then circulating concerning the extent of the horrors taking place under the Pol Pot regime, and raised doubts regarding the accuracy of the enormously high figures estimating how many had been killed. The extreme measures employed by Pol Pot were portrayed as typical of what occurs when an "ancient regime" is replaced. The great population transfers were necessitated, it as argued, by the country's inability to feed its large urban population.[107] By January 1979, the newsletter's line on this subject had altered drastically, reflecting changes in Soviet foreign policy. The Pol Pot regime now was seen as inhuman. The December 1978 Vietnamese invasion of Cambodia was praised. From this new perspective, Pathe suddenly came to view the forced movement of population in Cambodia as something pushed to absurd limits.[108]

A similar shift in attitude was apparent in Pathe's handling of events in Iran. *Synthesis* initially was supportive of the Khomeini regime, and spotlighted the role of the Marxists in bringing down the regime of the Shah.[109] Shortly thereafter, however, Khomeini turned against the Marxist groups, and *Synthesis* took a critical stance toward the new ruler in response to this policy.[110]

Defamation of Moscow's Ideological Opponents. The absence of a fine and delicate hand often can be seen in *Synthesis*. Nowhere was this more apparent than in the newsletter's attacks on ideological opponents within the Marxist-Leninist camp. Clearly manifest in these attacks were fears of the dissent and the challenges to the USSR that might be mounted by other Communist governments asserting the correctness of their ideological positions.

One of the principal targets, of course, was China. Pathe's criticisms of the Peking regime at first were careful. Earlier issues of the publication voiced the theme that China now follows the same road to economic development as does the USSR, suggesting the rejection of Mao's cultural revolution. By late in 1978, however, the criticisms leveled against Mao's economic, cultural, and political policies had become more vigorous. By March 1979, in the aftermath of China's attack on Vietnam, Pathe's strong charges against Peking had all the signs of having been composed in Moscow.[111] At that time, China was described as having "lived in the absurd in words and actions" for twenty years. Chinese foreign policy and the Chinese press were excoriated, and the attack on Vietnam was condemned. Pathe further accused China of having informed the United States of its intentions, and having received Washington's tacit approval for the attack on Vietnam. Finally, Pathe portrayed in bleak terms the Chinese demographic problem and the country's prospects for industrialization.

An article at the end of 1978 was critical of Rumania and Communist Party leader Nicolae Ceausescu. It attacked the Rumanian regime for its anti-Soviet positions and xenophobia. References were made to nepotism involving Ceausescu's wife, brother, and other figures—a practice, Pathe asserted, which is hardly tolerated elsewhere in the Communist world. The article discounted the significance of Rumania's alleged independence in foreign affairs, in view of the country's geographic proximity to the Soviet Union.[112]

Soviet dissidents and émigrés comprised another unconcealed object of attack and defamation. Here the Soviet hand appeared evident—either betraying a possible failure of judgment on the part of Pathe's Soviet handlers regarding how best to treat this theme, or reflecting panic in Moscow. Commentary was devoted to the failure of Soviet émigrés to integrate into Israeli life; and it was asserted that Soviet adults find it difficult to adjust to the capitalist world, since the "Homo Sovieticus" fashioned by the Soviet regime is a quite different being.[113] It appears that Moscow had lost patience with anti-Soviet attacks in the West stemming from Soviet dissidents.

Continuing this line of criticism, Pathe downplayed the revelations of the Czech defector Karel Kaplan, and warned of the dissemination of false information by Western intelligence services. Pathe also spoke of the lack of influence exerted by Soviet dissidents in the Soviet Union. The Western press chooses to ignore the truth of this situation, he charged, and prefers to live with its prejudices. Pathe then went on to assert that flattery in the West was turning Soviet émigrés into "wrecks" (*epaves*), 90 percent of whom cannot adapt to Western society.[114] In an article on the CPSU, *Synthesis* again criticized Soviet émigrés and dissidents, accusing them of presenting a false picture of the Communist Party and calling into question their impartiality. The same article described émigré opponents of the Soviet regime as "fish out of water" and "officers without troops," incapable of forming a real opposition. The only opposition in the USSR, Pathe stated, is found among isolated intellectuals.[115]

The pattern apparent in *Synthesis* of strong reaction to ideological issues, or to subjects touching upon the *raison d'etre* of a Communist society, was evident in articles concerning the anti-Marxist French philosophers known as "the new philosophers." The newsletter characterized their views as nihilistic, and asserted they were focused on secondary matters. Pathe commented, for example, that "the way they keep returning to the subject of the Gulag is laughable."[116] Another attack referred to their ignorance of real problems as "abysmal," their "elegant discourses" as displaying great confusion, and their rhetoric as anarchic. The article raised questions regarding how these philosophers can discourse on oppression in societies far away, and pronounced that the logical conclusion of their ideas is "political terrorism." In the USSR, it was added, the members of this school are laughed at.[117]

Another theme in *Synthesis* was the issue of human rights raised by the Carter Administration. During the Conference on Security and Cooperation in Europe (the "Helsinki Conference"), which began in 1977, Pathe warned that the Soviets would air the West's "dirty linen" in a massive way if the latter continued to interfere in what should be regarded as internal Soviet matters.[118] When confronting criticism of the USSR and its friends on such specific issues as human rights, an apparent defensive measure employed by Pathe involved discrediting the reliability and accuracy of the French media, and—more generally—the Western media. This tactic also served the transparent purpose of deflecting attacks by asserting the impeccability of the critic's moral credentials.

Pathe therefore stressed the thesis that the Western press is unreliable on many matters and is silent on others, and is subject to a wide variety of extraneous pressures (including those of circulation requirements). Reference was made to the venality of the French press, and to its past history of relations with foreign powers. The French press was called to account for a barrage of stories concerning human rights in distant countries characterized by differing cultures, where France could not hope to have any influence.[119]

Another comment referred to gaps in Western press information on the USSR which "reach the level of disinformation."[120] In discussing a United Nations Educational, Scientific, and Cultural Organization (UNESCO) resolution on the subject of press communications, Pathe discounted as dishonest Western arguments about the lack of freedom of the press in Soviet block countries.[121] Finally, *Synthesis* also carried complaints that the Western press lionizes Soviet dissidents and émigrés, and prefers not to seek the truth.[122]

SOVIET FORGERIES

From the earliest days of the Bolshevik regime, forged documents have been employed by Moscow to discredit and deceive opponents. For example, forgeries played an important role in the "Trust" operations of the 1920s, elaborate and highly successful schemes devised by Felix Dzerzhinsky (founding director of the Cheka) for luring important counterrevolutionaries back to their capture and death in Russia, and—later on—for discrediting anti-Soviet groups in Europe. The "Trust" also helped disseminate Moscow's message that the new Bolshevik regime was too strong to be subverted by "renegade" groups.

Dzerzhinsky in effect created a fake counterrevolutionary organization (known as the "Trust") for these purposes. Skilled agents were dispatched to Europe to approach émigré opposition leaders. To convince these leaders of the legitimacy of this organization, a number of tactics were employed, including forged letters, instructions, and agreements.[123]

During the years from 1960 to 1980, forged documents continued to play a role in Soviet covert activities; and forgeries appear to have been coordinated with other overt and covert techniques, and closely related to specific Soviet objectives. During the early 1960s and the latter half of the 1970s, many forged documents were targeted against the United States and NATO. Selected samples of forged materials from both periods, particularly those aimed at the United States, have been declassified by the CIA. They have been published in Congressional hearings, along with explanations of how each document came to be identified as a forgery.[124] As far as can be determined, these CIA assessments have not been challenged. (It should be noted that the CIA may not have made available all the forgeries in its possession, and the US government may not have discovered all the forgeries disseminated by the Soviets.)

As has been the case since the late 1950s with certain other Soviet disinformation tactics, forgeries are formulated and executed through Service A of the KGB's First Chief Directorate. In addition to conducting its own forgery operations, Service A also directs and supervises the forgeries and other disinformation activities that are carried out by the intelligence services of the East European satellites. Ladislav Bittman, a former Czech intelligence officer who specialized in disinformation operations, has described the relationship between the KGB and the bloc intelligence services as follows:[125]

> The East German, Czechoslovak, Polish, Hungarian, and Bulgarian services are subordinated formally to their governments, but they are directed mainly by the KGB. Moscow is informed about every operational detail of their activities . . . Russian advisors influence the planning of each operation and assess the results. No important decision is made without them.

During the period under examination in this study, many of the forgeries that were directed against the United States took the form of authentic-looking but false US government documents and communiqués. These falsifications fall into two general categories: (a) altered or distorted versions of actual US documents the Soviets have been able to obtain (usually through espionage), and (b) documents which are entirely fabricated. These anti-US forgeries are aimed at both the political elites and the general populations of the various target states.

Regardless of the type of forgery employed and the intended target, the general thrust of these falsified documents has been consistent. In using this technique, Soviet leaders apparently sought to portray the United States as the major threat to peace, to create suspicion and discord in relations between the United States and its West European allies, and to characterize US policy in the Third World as imperialistic. These themes are evident both in the forgeries which occurred in the early 1960s, and in those which have appeared since the mid-1970s.

Soviet Forgeries During the Late 1950s and the Early 1960s

During the late 1950s and the early 1960s, a number of forgeries designed to pass as official documents and communications of the US government were identified.[126] They followed three general patterns.

First, the United States was presented as the major threat to world peace. As was demonstrated in the previous chapter, this theme also dominated the overt propaganda in both *New Times* and *Pravda*'s "International Review" during 1961 and 1962. A false State Department directive ordering US diplomatic missions abroad to exert all possible efforts to sabotage negotiations for a summit conference serves as an illustration of how forgeries were used to emphasize this theme.[127] The forged State Department document was designed to mirror commentary appearing in Soviet overt propaganda during the early 1960s, which constantly asserted that the United States was doing everything possible to sabotage all negotiations with the USSR, especially on disarmament matters.

Another forgery related to Moscow's attempt to portray the United States as the major enemy of peace amplified the spring 1960 propaganda windfall resulting from the U-2 incident. A forged memorandum from US Air Attaché Emmens to Ambassador MacArthur in Tokyo outlined alleged secret plans of the American government to conceal U-2s in Japan for renewed flights over the USSR and China.[128]

Other forgeries singled out the US Strategic Air Command (SAC) as an important element of the dangers emanating from the United States. SAC personnel were portrayed as a highly psychotic group, capable of initiating a nuclear war at any moment. An example is provided by a forged letter purportedly from Assistant Secretary of Defense (Health and Medical) Frank Berry to the Secretary of Defense. The fabrication asserted that 67.3 percent of all SAC flight personnel were psychoneurotics, with such symptoms as phobias, unaccountable animosity, and irrational behavior. It further stated that "moral depression is a typical condition of all crew members making flights with atomic and H-bombs."[129] The fabricated letter from Berry was followed by a series of bogus letters ostensibly written by unidentified "neurotic US pilots" exhibiting these traits.[130]

A second group of forgeries was designed to reveal the imperialist plans and ambitions of the United States in the Third World. This thrust again paralleled a major theme appearing in Soviet overt propaganda. While many of these forgeries were targeted on the political elites of specific countries, others focused on a much wider audience. A fabricated letter from Nelson Rockefeller to President Dwight Eisenhower serves as an illustration. The letter, which appeared during the late 1950s, purportedly contained a plan for American manipulation of military and economic aid in an effort to gain world hegemony. A portion of the forgery read:[131]

> To put the policy in a nutshell—our policy must be . . . "global": i.e., include political, psychological, economic, military, and special methods integrated into one

whole. In other words, the task is to hitch all of our horses in a single team. . . . Provided all of the recommendations are carried out the result would be not only to strengthen the international position of the US as a whole but would also considerably facilitate the fulfillment of any military tasks that may confront the US in the future.

Examples of more narrowly-crafted fabrications include items ostensibly revealing American plans to manipulate the leaders of, and politics in, Third World nations. Evidence of Washington's aims in this area was "unveiled" in the form of forged cables from the American Embassy in Djakarta containing proposed plans to overthrow Indonesian President Sukarno.[132] Other forgeries purported to reveal American plots to depose Sihanouk of Cambodia and Nasser of Egypt.[133] Another false document contained instructions from the United States Information Service (USIS) advising that the officials of one Asian country should be pressured to verbally attack other Asian countries. Additionally, a forged letter from the Undersecretary of State to the US Ambassador in Leopoldville stated that the United States had successfully recruited Premier Moise Tshombe as an agent.[134]

Third, forgeries were used in an attempt to provoke discord among members of the Western alliance. A letter ostensibly sent from the Head of the Political Section of the US Embassy in West Germany to the State Department, for example, was intended to show that the United States looked favorably on neo-Nazi organizations in West Germany.[135] This fabrication thus amplified the Nazi-revanchist theme that dominated Soviet overt propaganda directed at West Germany during this period.

Soviet Forgeries Since the Mid-1970s

Since 1976, the main thrust of Soviet forgeries has been directed at compromising the position of the United States in Western Europe, and at provoking disharmony in the Western alliance. These falsifications have stressed the American nuclear threat to

Europe, the plans and involvement of the United States in manipulating internal European politics, and American measures devised to damage the economies of the European states. A second focus has concentrated on undermining US relations with Third World countries, especially in the Middle East. Finally, it appears that a few forgeries have been intended to deflect attention from Soviet activities outside the borders of the USSR.

In the previous chapter it was observed that a key theme of Soviet overt propaganda during the 1976–1979 period was the charge that in the case of nuclear war in Europe, the United States planned to sacrifice its NATO allies in order to save itself. This theme also appears in Soviet forgeries, in a more crude and provocative manner. During 1980, for example, Moscow began to resurrect a number of forged American and NATO documents that had first been used in Europe during the late 1960s and the early 1970s. The introduction to this collection of forgeries, which were published in a single pamphlet by an unidentified group in England under the title "Holocaust Again in Europe," followed the same Soviet propaganda themes aimed at sowing discord among the member states of NATO.

In attempting to invalidate the basis for NATO's plans for modernization of its intermediate-range nuclear forces, the authors of the pamphlet noted: "NATO modernization strategy turns essentially on two beliefs—first, the Warsaw Pact has a superiority in the European theatre and, second, that it seeks political objectives which could only be secured by use of that superiority."[136] According to the authors, "neither belief is valid. The essential balance between NATO and Warsaw Pact forces in Europe is a matter of record." The second belief was characterized as "even more laughable," and the authors went on to argue that "militarily, the political advantage theory collapses because it is based on the false premise that tactical nuclear strikes can comprise the sum total of a nuclear war."[137]

These assertions led to the reiteration of another key theme of Soviet overt propaganda: "there is no Soviet threat, there is a real American threat to Europe."[138] This threat was said to derive from an American strategy for the European theatre that is dominated by preparation for war, rather than for the defense of Europe, and from Washington's view of "nuclear war confined to Europe as no more than the ultimate extension of the 'little wars' of the post-WWII variety."[139]

Furthermore, the forgery purported to demonstrate clearly that "when a European-based nuclear war is effectively unbridled," the leaders of the United States "believe they can escape the consequences and, most importantly, they believe they can reap all the possible benefits."[140] The Soviet Union, on the other hand, aimed to convince the West European members of NATO that "the installation of nuclear medium-range missiles in Europe is a trap for the Europeans themselves, one from which only the Americans can gain." Such an installation would mean for Europe "being burnt, blasted, and shocked out of existence in the process."[141]

A number of other forgeries provided variations on the theme of American willingness to sacrifice its NATO allies. An authentic, unclassified US government map was misrepresented, for example, so that the Pentagon could be charged with targeting Austrian cities and facilities for nuclear destruction in the event of war in Europe.[142] A fabricated letter ostensibly written by the US Defense Attaché in Rome contained language denying "rumors suggesting the death of children in Naples could be due to chemical or biological substances stored at . . . American bases near Naples."[143] A forged letter allegedly sent in 1976 to NATO Secretary General Joseph Luns by Supreme Commander Alexander Haig stated that NATO strategy demands further attention to "the limited use of US nuclear forces in Europe in an emergency."[144] A bogus letter was written on official NATO stationery bearing the forged signature of the NATO Secretary General. In the letter, the US Ambassador to NATO was informed that the Belgian Defense Ministry had compiled files on journalists who opposed deployment of the neutron bomb, implying that they would be punished. (This forgery appeared during the massive Soviet campaign of overt propaganda against the neutron weapon.)[145]

A second group of Soviet forgeries directed against the

United States and NATO since the mid-1970s purported to provide "evidence" of direct and unscrupulous American attempts to manipulate the internal politics of Washington's European allies. A case in point is a 1978 fabrication entitled "Intelligence Collection Requirements." This document, which first appeared in a Greek newspaper (*To Vima*), allegedly presented instructions from the US Defense Intelligence Agency in connection with American spying on 43 Greek political parties and organizations.[146] At approximately the same time, Greek opposition leader Andreas Papandreou presented to the Greek Parliament a copy of what turned out to be a forged State Department telegram purportedly outlining an American policy favoring Ankara in the Greek-Turkish dispute.[147] The purpose behind both forgeries apparently was to create strains in the relations between Greece and the United States, thereby weakening the coherence of the NATO alliance.

Greece continued as a target of Soviet forgeries during the early 1980s. A falsified letter from Undersecretary of State William Clark to the American Ambassador to Greece, Monteagle Stearns, ostensibly recommended that Stearns should utilize a study sponsored by the State Department on the "Current Political Situation" in Greece. The study, purportedly endorsed by Clark, suggested that the United States might support a military coup in Greece in order to preserve its military bases.[148] The relationship of the United States with Spain also became a subject of Soviet fabrications, and a forged letter from President Reagan to King Juan Carlos was designed to reveal to the latter that a number of his close advisors opposed Spain's entry into NATO.[149] Finally, in addition to these forgeries emphasizing US manipulation of European politics (and the forgeries stressing the American nuclear threat to Europe, described earlier), a few falsifications appeared during this period which allegedly revealed American plans to manipulate and create crises within the European economies.[150]

A second major thrust of Soviet forgeries in the years since 1976 has been an attempt to undermine the policies and reputation of the United States in the Third World. A series of statements against Egypt's President Sadat were falsely attributed to important US government officials, including Vice President Walter Mondale and Secretary of State Cyrus Vance, in an attempt to hinder US-Egyptian relations.[151] Similar forged documents were aimed at undermining US policies in Latin America and Africa.[152]

A third major category of forgeries which appeared during this period can be seen as attempts on the part of Moscow to justify or to redirect international attention away from certain Soviet actions outside the borders of the USSR. For example, a forged 1980 State Department telegram, supposedly found in the aftermath of a fire at the American Embassy in Islamabad, made the claim that a regular CIA courier to former Afghan President Hafizullah Amin had disappeared.[153] The purpose of the fabrication apparently was to link Amin to the CIA, a charge that had been made in the Soviet media after Moscow's invasion of Afghanistan. This forgery was followed in 1981 by the appearance of an altered, unclassified CIA map of Afghanistan. The story accompanying the map, which first appeared in an Indian newspaper, alleged that the map provided evidence of CIA involvement with the Afghan guerrillas. Purportedly contained in the map were specific targets selected by the CIA for destruction by the guerrillas (e.g., power stations, airfields, mines, etc.).[154]

This brief examination suggests that since 1976, Soviet forgeries have become more sophisticated and of a higher quality than the forgeries which appeared in the late 1950s and the early 1960s. Additionally, the main target of these efforts has shifted somewhat, with more emphasis devoted in recent years to relations between the United States and its NATO allies. Other important aspects of this area of Soviet active measures have remained basically consistent, however. First, Soviet forgeries have continued to parallel—although in a more crude and slanderous manner—major themes of overt propaganda carried in *New Times*, *Pravda*, and Radio Moscow. Second, the forgeries studied by the present authors apparently were intended to serve important objectives of Soviet foreign policy. (Certainly this was the case with respect to the recent series of fabrications directed toward provoking suspicion and dissension in the relations among the NATO allies.)

Whether or not a forged document is acquired, accepted, and published in the non-Communist media as authentic continues to depend on the content of the material, the method whereby it surfaces, and the overall sophistication of the document. As far as can be determined from the forgeries reviewed above, the Soviet record in this respect is mixed. In some cases, such as the forged Presidential letter to King Juan Carlos of Spain, press commentary either ignored the document or noted that it was bogus. Other falsified documents, however, received varying degrees of press coverage.

One of the most successful Soviet efforts involved a forged US Army Field Manual (FM 30–31B). This manual purportedly provided guidance to Army intelligence personnel regarding interference in the affairs of the host country, the subversion of foreign officials and military officers, and the use of extreme leftist organizations to safeguard American interests in friendly nations where it appears that Communists may enter the government.[155] First mentioned in 1975 in a Turkish newspaper, this document was reprinted in two Spanish publications in 1978, and since that time has been the subject of articles published in more than twenty countries, including the United States.

CHAPTER V

INTERVIEWS WITH FORMER SOVIET BLOC INTELLIGENCE OFFICERS

THIS CHAPTER CONTAINS interviews, conducted separately, with two former Soviet bloc intelligence officers who specialized in active measures during the 1960s and 1970s.

Ladislav Bittman served as a career Czech intelligence officer from 1954 until 1968. During this period, he spent eight years abroad directing and recruiting spies, and for two years (1964–1966) held the post of Deputy Chief of the Disinformation Department (Department Eight) of the Czech intelligence service. From 1966 to 1968, Bittman operated in Vienna under diplomatic cover as a press attaché of the Czechoslovakian Diplomatic Mission, attempting to manipulate the Austrian press and directing agents of influence. In August 1968, in the aftermath of the invasion of Czechoslovakia by Warsaw Pact forces, Bittman crossed the West German border and asked US authorities for asylum. He now lives in the United States.

Stanislav Levchenko worked for the International Department of the CPSU Central Committee from 1965 to 1971, assisting with the direction of Soviet international front organizations. He joined the KGB in 1971, and in the fall of 1972 became a case officer of the Japanese Desk of the 7th Department of the KGB's First Chief Directorate. In February 1975, Levchenko was assigned to the Tokyo residency of the KGB to work in political intelligence; and in early 1979, he became the active chief of the Tokyo KGB residency's active measures group. In October 1979, Levchenko contacted US officials in Japan and requested asylum. Like Bittman, he now lives in the United States.

These two former specialists in active measures provide another level of information regarding how the Soviet bloc sought to influence international events during the 1960s and the 1970s. Both have published and lectured about their experiences, and are considered reliable.[1] They are a unique source for the student of Soviet foreign policy behavior.

The authors conducted what in social science terms are called "semi-structured" interviews with Bittman and Levchenko separately during January and February 1983. In both cases, a systematic series of questions was asked concerning the manner in which active measures were formulated and conducted in the field. The questions addressed to Bittman and Levchenko concentrated on the organization, control, and evaluation of active measures, and on the specific procedures utilized for conducting influence operations. Additionally, Levchenko was asked to discuss his experiences with Soviet overt propaganda and international front organizations. The responses of Bittman and Levchenko not only provide important insights into the ways in which Soviet bloc intelligence conducts active measures, but also provide—for the first time—information on how Moscow evaluates the effectiveness of these efforts.

INTERVIEW WITH LADISLAV BITTMAN, FORMER CZECH INTELLIGENCE OFFICER

For eight years during the late 1950s and the early 1960s, you recruited and directed agents of influence in Europe. What types of elites did you target, recruit, and direct? How many agents did you handle?

In the field, during the 1960s, agents-of-influence operations were the duty of the intelligence staff officer. At that time, although there was a disinformation department in Prague, it did not have its own officers in the field specifically for conducting influence operations. So, as an officer in the field, I targeted all major government offices and ministries, political parties, opinion leaders, and so on, first of all for intelligence collection. Within these target categories, we also conducted influence operations. I personally focused on political figures and journalists. At any given time, I had four or five agents, but not all would be conducting influence operations.

What was the political outlook of these agents? Where would you place them on the political spectrum?

The objective, of course, is not to recruit solely on the left, but rather across the political spectrum. Let me use West Germany as an example, for I had quite a lot of operational experience there. Czech intelligence recruited agents in all the political parties, including both the Social Democrats and the Christian Democrats. The Social Democratic Party was deeply penetrated, but we also had agents among the Christian Democrats. Furthermore, we focused our efforts not only on the federal structure, but also on the state parliaments.

What were your basic techniques for recruiting these agents?

Recruitment is a two-to-three year process that involves extensive background investigation to assess whether the target is vulnerable. During my years, blackmail was quite widely used. Ideology was of less importance during the 1960s in comparison with the 1950s. Money was very important, and almost every case with which I was familiar included payments. Still, in many cases a blackmail angle was employed in hooking the target, but this was carried out in a careful and not a heavy-handed way. This aspect was handled more subtly in the 1960s than in the 1950s. However, case officers also would seek to establish common interests and concerns with the target, especially once the relationship had been established. In West Germany, for example, if you were working with an individual on the political right, German nationalism, US domination and manipulation of West Germany, and similar acceptable themes were stressed.

Of the agents you directed, how many knew you were a Czech intelligence officer? Did they believe your cover?

In my own experience, almost every agent with whom I was connected knew I was a Czech intelligence officer—maybe not at first, but certainly once the relationship had developed. My own cover was within the Czech foreign ministry. However, a number of other institutions were likewise used. Every institution with foreign activities was employed, including trade organizations and associations, transportation organizations, journalist groups, and social groupings (e.g., victims of Nazi aggression). During the early 1960s, increasing stress was placed in the professional development of the intelligence officer on becoming knowledgeable regarding the cover which would be employed. For example, the intelligence officer who would use the Czech press agency as a cover was expected to learn all aspects of it before going abroad. Other types of cover likewise required similar professional training.

Let us focus on journalists. You stated in your 1980 Congressional testimony that during your time in the field, you were in contact with the director of a national television network in Western Europe. What other kinds of journalists did you recruit?

I did not personally make the recruitment approach, but instead conducted the spotting and assessing of the target. Someone else would conduct the actual recruitment. Therefore, if the operation failed, I would not be exposed. We recruited many more journalists on the left of the political spectrum than in the center or on the right. A range of techniques was used to hook the individual. Subtle forms of blackmail were used in conjunction with money and the interaction of personalities (developing common interests and concerns). As with all recruitments, the objective was to establish a web of complicity that encircled the agent. Money was used to keep the person happy and producing.

How did you use these journalist recruits? Were they used only to publish articles? What were the themes you focused on?

The primary responsibility of these journalists was to publish articles and stories, but these pieces did not emphasize support for Soviet policy. Rather, the major focus concentrated on undermining the United States and NATO, and on creating rifts between West Germany and France or between the United States and its allies. The principal theme argued that the NATO alliance was disintegrating because the United States was militaristic, dangerous, and not sensitive to European needs. For example, in West Germany the United States was charged with ignoring German heritage and culture during the post-war occupation, and with forcing alien institutions and political culture on the German people. West Germany, in turn, was presented to the French and to other Europeans as harboring strong Nazi tendencies, and it was claimed that many war criminals had been reinstated into positions of political power in the West German government. This was presented as extremely dangerous for all of Europe.

How did you get the journalists to produce? Did you provide completed articles for them to publish?

I knew of no situation in which completed articles were passed to an agent. This would be operationally awkward, and might end up revealing the association. The reason I say this is because it is extremely difficult to copy someone else's writing style. I did provide guidelines for the agent to follow. These consisted of a two- or three-page outline of objectives and themes to be covered in a given article. After I had provided these guidelines, the agent then would produce the story. Sometimes I would include materials and information he could draw upon.

Did the journalists you directed serve other purposes? Did you use them for influence operations against other journalists, political figures, or other important associates?

All agents, including journalists, were employed for intelligence collection. They frequently had access to confidential information that could be quite useful. As for influence operations, during my time we used only a few journalists for this purpose. I would say that the majority of the journalists we directed were not used for influence operations. Only the most reliable individuals, and those with useful connections, were used in this capacity.

How about recruitment? Did you use journalists to recruit other journalists?

I would say that it was very rare indeed when an agent could be used in this capacity. He could be used, however, to identify potential targets. Furthermore, if he was acquainted with a target, the agent could assist in gathering the kinds of information necessary to determine whether the target was vulnerable, and how you might catch him.

How closely did headquarters monitor and evaluate journalist operations? What criteria were used to measure effectiveness?

In the case of journalists, the criteria tended to be straightforward: the number of articles published, the quality of these articles, and where they appeared (i.e., whether they were published in a major newspaper). These were the general measures employed. Whether or not the articles persuaded the intended targets is much more difficult to determine, and is quite subjective. Evaluating other types of active measures operations was equally subjective. A forgery is a good example, as is overt propaganda. The immediate impact of these operations is often unclear. During my time, there was no highly developed system for measuring the immediate impact of disinformation exercises. All such operations were evaluated in terms of their cumulative effect on the target over time. This is the way Moscow and Prague approached such questions during the 1960s.

Let me ask you about the operations of the Disinformation

Department (Department Eight) of the Czech intelligence service. When you were Deputy Chief of the Department in Prague (1964–1966), what was your relationship with officers in the field?

First of all, the Disinformation Department during the mid-1960s had no operatives in the field. Neither did it have authority over the territorial operational department officers who, in addition to their collection duties, did conduct active measures in the field. We could review and analyze their operations, make recommendations, and formulate suggestions, but we could not direct their activities. It should be remembered that active measures were initiated by the territorial departments, as an added function to their primary collection responsibilities. Department Eight had no operatives abroad with sole responsibility for conducting active measures.

The sole authority held by Department Eight over the territorial departments was its regular annual evaluation of the active measures conducted throughout the intelligence apparatus, and its criticism of departments which had not been sufficiently active. So, we could critically analyze and evaluate programs and make recommendations, but we had no operational control at the territorial level. Furthermore, since we did not have detailed knowledge of the agents recruited in the territorial departments, our recommendations took the form of more generalized guidelines. Thus, during the mid-1960s we could not effectively make use of the resources of the territorial departments in conducting active measures.

Could Department Eight initiate any active measures of its own?

During my time, we generally focused on forgeries, black propaganda, disinformation, rumors, and intrigues. (At that time, for the reasons discussed above, we were not involved with influence operations.) Basically, each of these special operations sought to deceive the enemy or victim by feeding him false information that would lead to the conclusions we wished him to reach. In the 1960s, the Czech intelligence service directed operations of this sort against such developing nations as Egypt and Algeria. The material utilized included forged data on various anti-Arab operations and on subversive activities planned by the United States, Great Britain, and other European nations. The objective was to deepen Arab distrust of the Western world, and draw the Arab states closer to Moscow and the Eastern bloc.

Similar operations were directed against relations among the NATO allies. In 1964 I was involved in an extremely successful action (Operation Neptune) conducted against West Germany. It was announced that important Nazi documents, including lists of Nazi agents in Eastern Europe, had been discovered in a lake on the West German-Czech border. The goal was to paralyze the activities of West German intelligence. They were said to be working with former Nazi agents—people in Eastern Europe who had collaborated with the Nazi regime. It was hoped that these so-called lists would force West German intelligence to break contact with these persons. The operation was considered most successful.[2]

Let us return to influence operations. When you were stationed in West Germany, you directed agents in the German parliament. How did you use these agents? Did you employ them for influence operations?

As I stated above, the intelligence officer in the field conducted influence operations in addition to his primary collection responsibilities. However, there were cases in West Germany in which recruited agents in parliament were employed for influence operations. For example, I was the case officer for Alfred Frenzel, a Social Democratic member of the Bundestag. Frenzel was a member of several parliamentary committees, including the Committee for Defense. He was used to obtain information about the defense capabilities of West Germany and NATO, and also was directed to influence certain decisions, if possible, in the interest of the USSR. We instructed him on how to react and on what positions to take during meetings of parliament.

Broadly speaking, what were the major targets of the Czech Disinformation Department when you were Deputy Chief in the mid-1960s?

Based on plans prepared in the 1960s by Moscow and assigned to the Czech service, the primary target was the United States. The objective was to damage the United States wherever possible, and to weaken its position in Western Europe. We sought to create rifts between the United States and its West European allies, as well as among the various members of NATO. For example, we sought to cause disagreements between the United States and its NATO allies about the military strength of the Warsaw Pact countries. This military disinformation, in my estimation, has developed into a very important aspect of current Soviet disinformation activities. Additionally, we also focused on the Third World, and on American relations with these new nations. Again, the objective of Czech disinformation was to cause rifts, and to discredit US policies and programs in the Third World.

How detailed were the directions Czech intelligence received from Moscow? How specific were these directions in an operational sense? How close was Moscow's oversight?

Let me answer this on two levels. First of all, during the 1960s, we received guidance and objectives from Moscow center, articulated through KGB advisors who were present at all important Czech intelligence service staff levels. These broad policy objectives directed Czech intelligence to develop programs aimed at damaging the United States whenever and wherever possible, to weaken the position of the United States and Western Europe, to create new rifts within the NATO alliance, and to cause breaches between the United States and the developing countries. Our staff then would meet and devise specific proposals and plans for implementing these guidelines in the field. Before these instructions were sent to the field, however, we consulted with the KGB officer assigned to our staff.

Were you required to clear all plans through this KGB officer? Could he reject your plans?

Yes, he was able to reject these directives. In my own case, the relationship was businesslike. I would consult with him, and he might make changes and recommendations. However, it was always clear that he could say "no" to the plans. This staff oversight took place on a daily basis.

In the field, was there room for innovation? Could you make changes in orders and plans and then carry them out, or did everything require approval in Prague?

There was room, of course, for initiative and innovation among officers in the field. It was necessary, however, to clear changes and plans with headquarters. This was a time-consuming process, which sometimes caused opportunities to be missed. In other words, a Czech field officer had to send all plans or changes back to Prague for review by the territorial operational department (and the department's Soviet advisor). This procedure applied to all active measures proposals.

For the officer in the field conducting influence and other active measures operations, how closely were these operations evaluated? What criteria are used to evaluate operations?

Broadly speaking, each field officer was evaluated on an annual basis. Headquarters would examine all your activities, how well you were doing with the agents you were directing, what these agents had achieved, and how far you could go with each. With regard to active measures, you were evaluated in terms of the number of operations proposed and conducted, and the success of these actions. Evaluative criteria did exist for these operations, although in certain cases these criteria were quite subjective. For example, as I noted earlier, influence operations conducted through journalists had specific measurements of effectiveness. These included the number of articles published, how effectively they were written, and where they were published. In the case of a forgery, on the other hand, the criteria for effectiveness were much more subjective. This also was true of other techniques.

It is important to note, however, that the Communist approach to questions of effectiveness is different from the Western approach. The Communist concern focuses more on the overall cumulative effect over time. Furthermore, the Communist view of time is much different from the Western view. Hence, Communist leaders do not emphasize the specific effectiveness of each type of active measures operation, many of which are difficult to evaluate, to the extent this is emphasized in the West. In the Communist view, it is the cumulative impact that is important. This, at least, was my experience during the 1960s.

Many in the West discount Soviet and Eastern bloc use of agents of influence, international front organizations, and other active measures operations as either not very important or not very effective. Based on your experience in the 1960s, how would you respond to this assertion?

When the size and growth during the 1960s of the overall Soviet and Eastern bloc effort in this area are considered, it is clear that Moscow viewed this component of strategy as quite important. The resources and personnel devoted to these operations were rapidly expanding. Developments during the 1970s, in my opinion, confirm the importance of these activities in Moscow's view. How effective had these efforts been in the overall scheme of things? Look at Soviet influence and presence in the world in 1980 as compared with 1955. Furthermore, my own study of Soviet military disinformation, economic games, use of refugee operations (recently Cubans), and influence operations leads me to the conclusion that these measures have played an important part in the overall Soviet effort directed against the United States and NATO.

INTERVIEW WITH STANISLAV LEVCHENKO, FORMER KGB INTELLIGENCE OFFICER

You handled journalists in Japan. How were you able to recruit them? What types of journalists did you seek for conducting active measures?

First of all, recruitment is a very long and complicated process. It takes two to four years to complete a recruitment and have the agent producing for you. To accomplish this, you use all the tools of professional tradecraft. A thorough background investigation takes place to determine what angles to use in recruiting the target. A KGB officer generally focuses on recruiting two kinds of journalists. One type is the specialist in a particular subject area who possesses both sensitive information and connections with key individuals.

What kinds of specialists does the KGB focus on?

Writers who have developed an expertise in various aspects of political, economic, or military affairs are sought. I concentrated on political specialists. Such an agent can be of assistance in a number of ways. He can produce stories, of course, supporting Soviet objectives with respect to a particular issue. Additionally, he may have access to confidential information which he can collect for you. Finally, because he is a specialist, he may know and interact with other elites. You then can task the agent to conduct various influence operations against these persons. Four of the agents I handled in Japan were prominent journalists. They had high-level contacts in the Socialist Party and the Liberal Democratic Party, and among government officials, including members of the Cabinet of Ministers. The journalists provided secret government information and documents. I also had them conduct various influence operations against these government officials.

What was the second category of journalist you focused on recruiting?

The second type of desired journalist is the individual with a wide following, or one associated with a newspaper with a wide distribution. One of the agents the KGB directed in Japan was a close confidant of the owner of a major Japanese newspaper with a daily circulation of three million copies. He was used to implement a variety of active measures against that newspaper.

Could you be a little more specific about the methods of recruitment used, and the political views of the agents of influence you directed? How many agents did you handle?

Once the decision has been made to approach a journalist or a member of another elite group, various methods of tradecraft are used. The specifics are determined on a case-by-case basis. Let me outline a model case for you. Generally, the idea is to find some common ground or interest upon which you can agree, and then establish a personal relationship with the target. This approach can be applied to targets across the political spectrum. For those on the left, the common interest might be cast in ideological terms. For those on the right, however, the common interest may be a particular issue. For example, a target might be very pro-Taiwan and in opposition to closer relations between Japan and the People's Republic of China. The common ground here is obvious, and a deal could be made on this issue. If this individual were a journalist, I would assist him by providing money, moral support and encouragement, and possibly information and materials.

What other methods are used in recruitment? Is blackmail used to recruit an agent and keep him active?

While establishing a personal relationship and a common interest is of the utmost importance, money also is useful. Certain individuals, even those who are anti-Soviet, will work for you solely for money. Money is a very persuasive tool. On the other hand, I did not find blackmail to be a useful technique. Of course, it has been used by the KGB. Personally I did not like blackmail, however, because I felt it could drive the agent into the hands of the target nation's counterintelligence branch.

What were the political views of the agents you handled in Japan? How many agents did you direct?

Roughly, about one third of the agents I handled were socialists and Marxist in outlook. Another third could be characterized as neutral, or in the political center. The final third were individuals on the right side of the political spectrum. By 1979, I was handling 10 agents and developmental contacts, with whom I had 20 to 25 clandestine meetings a month. In the Tokyo residency, there were 5 case officers conducting active measures through 25 agents of influence. The overall number of KGB officers in the Tokyo residency was approximately 50 to 60 officers.

Did most of the agents you handled understand your real identity? Were they aware that you were a KGB officer?

I would say that the majority of them did not know this. They believed I was a *New Times* correspondent, and not a KGB intelligence officer.

Did you provide the journalists you handled with material to publish? In other words, did you give them actual stories and articles?

In my own case, I provided guidelines, themes, and information, and then had the agent produce the article. I did not believe it would be wise to provide him with the entire article ready for publication. The reason behind my thinking was that each journalist has a particular style and method, and an article produced by me, or written back in Moscow, might stand out and tip off the counterintelligence of the target country. In general, you provide guidelines, themes, and objectives. You make suggestions, and discuss how the agent might implement and accomplish the objectives.

Were you able to get the agents you handled to recruit other agents, in addition to carrying out active measures operations?

It is very rare to have an agent who can actually carry out a recruitment. It happens, but not very often. It is much more common to have an agent assist you in spotting or identifying a possible recruitment. Once a potential target is spotted, you begin the lengthy process of assessing the individual to determine whether and how to approach him. Primarily, the agents I directed assisted me in this area by spotting possible targets for recruitment.

How did you determine whether to assign a particular task to one of your agents, and what approach he should take in conducting an operation?

As I mentioned above, active measures operations in Japan were based on directives we received from Moscow. We often received these on a daily basis, three to five directives at a time. Usually, the active measures case officers meet with the group chief to determine how best to implement the directives. Once the plan is decided on, you generally check back with Moscow for approval. This is not necessary for every action, but it is necessary for most of them.

What, in outline form, were the overall objectives of Moscow's active measures operations conducted against Japan during the time you were stationed in Tokyo?

The first priority was to prevent further development of US-Japanese cooperation, and to provoke distrust between Japan and the United States on economic, political, and military issues. A second goal was to hinder good relations between Japan and the People's Republic of China, and to prevent the creation of a Washington-Peking-Tokyo triangle. A third objective was to create a pro-Soviet lobby among prominent Japanese politicians (through penetration of the Liberal Democratic and Socialist Parties), leading to closer economic and political ties between the Soviet Union and Japan and the creation of a political monopoly in the Japanese parliament. The Japanese government likewise was to be persuaded through the use of high-ranking agents of influence, business leaders, and the mass media. These were among the leading objectives.

Please outline, if you can, the Soviet KGB effort in Japan during the years you were assigned there. Who were the most effective agents?

The KGB had a network of approximately 200 recruited agents in Japan, utilized by political intelligence, external counter-intelligence, and the scientific and technological intelligence of the First Chief Directorate. Among the most effective agents were a former member of the government's Cabinet of Ministers, who headed a major parliamentary public organization; several major officials of the Socialist Party; a prominent scholar on the People's Republic of China who had close contacts with government officials; and several members of the parliament. In my own case, the most important influence agents I directed were journalists.

Our assessment of New Times *demonstrates that a major part of its focus has been directed at attacking, denigrating, and criticizing the United States and NATO. You used* New Times *as a means of cover while serving as a KGB officer in Japan. Did you also write for* New Times? *On what themes did you concentrate? Did you focus at all on the United States and NATO?*

First of all, your assessment that the major focus of *New Times* is the United States and NATO is correct. However, as a *New Times* correspondent, my job was not to carry out overt propaganda; this was only my cover. My principal responsibility as a KGB officer was to recruit Japanese journalists, parliamentarians, and other elites for conducting various types of active measures. The KGB uses *New Times* for such activities. In the mid-1970s, *New Times* had twelve foreign correspondents, of which ten were KGB officers. However, of the other two, one was involved in a variety of activities with the International Department (ID). During my time, the two so-called "clean" correspondents were assigned to the United States and West Germany.

Still, to make your journalistic cover believable, didn't you produce stories? Or were these prepared for you back in Moscow?

The general rule is that most KGB officers under journalistic cover do not write in the field. Stories are filed on their behalf. My case in Japan was somewhat unusual. I actually sent one or two articles back to *New Times* each month. Two reasons may explain this. First, I had an extensive understanding of Asia because of my postgraduate studies. Second, *New Times* had no one at its headquarters who was knowledgeable about Japan. To return to your earlier question, the themes covered in these stories were related, in many instances, to the United States. I had a degree of freedom regarding what to write, but this was within certain broad categories. Thus, in my writing the issues of US militarism, economic problems, and imperialism were related to Japan and Asia. In many ways, these subjects reflected the major objectives of Soviet active measures in Japan—including the prevention of a further deepening of US-Japanese cooperation, and the provoking of distrust in US-Japanese economic, political, and military circles.

Let us pursue this question of journalistic cover a little further. How extensive was your training as a journalist? Does the KGB emphasize that one should become an expert in the activities used for cover?

In my own case, the final stage of preparation for my assignment to Japan consisted of spending almost one year with *New Times* in Moscow. I was expected to improve my journalistic skills, to study the mechanisms of editorial work, and to publish several articles. Thus, when I went to Japan, I would easily move into the journalistic community and carry out my real assignment. I had genuine journalistic experience, and this made my cover believable. This is not an unusual experience. The KGB prepares its officers in this manner.

Besides journalistic cover, what other forms of cover are used extensively by the KGB for conducting active measures?

The foreign trade ministry, which is involved in numerous economic and business ventures throughout the world and sends many officials overseas, also is of great importance for the KGB. As is true in the field of journalism, the KGB officer designated for this kind of cover learns all about it before being assigned abroad.

Since you are familiar with New Times, *let me ask you about its major targets. Whom do the Soviets seek to reach through this publication?*

New Times propaganda in large part is directed against foreign elites. In Western Europe, this includes academics, journalists, political leaders, and so on. These are the kinds of individuals, the Soviets know, who read the magazine and are influenced by it. Additionally, *New Times* sets the line on various issues for foreign Communist parties. Although *Problems of Peace and Socialism* also serves this purpose, it only comes out once a month. *New Times*, on the other hand, appears weekly. Finally, *New Times* also is used for internal propaganda directed at the population of the Soviet Union. *New Times*, in other words, is directed against both foreign and domestic audiences.

While we are on the subject of overt propaganda, let me ask you about the International Information Department (IID, which was created in 1978. Why was this CPSU Central Committee department established? Was Moscow dissatisfied with the coordination and performance of the overt propaganda effort?

First of all, I believe that the importance of the IID is overstated in the West. The IID is not on an equal footing with the International Department (ID). While it is true that the IID has responsibility for improving the timing, responsiveness, and coordination of the major overt propaganda channels of the USSR, this function was seen as necessary for internal audiences first and foreign audiences second. In other words, Moscow's dissatisfaction was with internal effectiveness. Furthermore, the IID does not set propaganda themes. This is more the responsibility of the ID (under the direction of the Politburo and the Central Committee). For instance, it is the ID—and not the IID—that directs and sets the themes to be covered in *New*

Times. The responsibility of the IID is to coordinate the various overt propaganda channels for internal and external audiences.

Based on your work with the International Department, please outline, if you will, how Moscow maintains influence over the international front organizations. How closely are these activities directed and monitored in the field?

First of all, Moscow does not influence the international fronts. Rather, it controls these organizations, through the ID. The main products of the fronts (appeals, conferences, publications, etc.) are decided on and crafted by the ID. For example, the Soviet Afro-Asian Solidarity Committee (AASC), under the close guidance of the International Department, manipulates the Afro-Asian People's Solidarity Organization (AAPSO). Likewise, the Soviet Peace Fund, also an active tool of the ID, is responsible for manipulating the World Peace Council. In each case, the activities of these organizations are directed toward supporting Soviet objectives. One way control is maintained is through domination of the leadership organs of these organizations. For instance, the majority of the AAPSO's presidential council is controlled by the Soviet Afro-Asian Solidarity Committee. Thus, all activities of the AAPSO are managed by the ID.

How does the ID control the activities of the local affiliates of the AAPSO and the WPC? Is this more difficult?

Depending on the situation, it may be more difficult. One frequently-used channel of control is through the local Communist party, which often is also controlled and directed by the ID. The US Peace Council is a case in point. Local arrangements and control also may be exerted through local KGB assets under covert direction.

What would be an example of an actual campaign or action directed by the ID against the United States?

The Vietnam Support Committee, a department of the Soviet AASC, helped to direct the AAPSO's anti-Vietnam War campaign on a worldwide basis. One of its programs was to use American deserters for international propaganda spectaculars. The AASC handled these deserters once they got to the USSR. The KGB also was involved, and established a route of escape for the deserters through Japan. To assist in this, the KGB penetrated the Japanese Vietnam Peace Committee, a very active organization consisting of intellectuals. In addition to the AAPSO, the WPC was very active in promoting Soviet propaganda against US involvement in Vietnam.

How do the fronts receive funding?

Again, this depends on whether you are talking about the international front itself, or about a regional or local organ of the front. In the case of the WPC, funding comes directly through the Soviet Peace Fund—which is to say, through the ID. The Soviet AASC provides a similar channel to the AAPSO. The AAPSO then may use this funding to conduct various activities specified by the ID, or to fund other organizations, such as so-called national liberation movements in the Third World. Funding to local affiliates of the WPC or the AAPSO, or to other international fronts, goes from the ID to the local Communist party by way of a KGB channel. This is one route for local assistance.

The major bureaucratic elements for formulating overt and covert propaganda are the ID and the KGB. In the field, do representatives of these bodies work closely together to coordinate activities, or is this all set out in Moscow? How are orders received, and how specific are they?

First of all, in foreign active measures operations, the major actors are the ID and the KGB. The IID plays a very minor role in conducting these activities. Its work is carried out in the Soviet Union. In the field, we generally would receive, on a weekly (and sometimes on a daily) basis, guidelines from Moscow regarding the various themes and activities we were to carry out. These orders could be quite detailed or only broad guidelines, depending on the issue. For long-term projects with which we all were familiar and on which we all had worked—for example, the anti-neutron weapon campaign or other major campaigns directed at denigrating the reputation of the United States—the orders we received were simply guidelines. Of course, we would meet as a staff to discuss how to implement these orders.

Is there room for innovation? Could you make changes in the orders, and then carry them out?

In our staff meetings we could recommend changes in orders and guidelines, and there was a great deal of room for innovation. However, in most cases these plans were sent back to Moscow for review. You generally would not take the initiative without first receiving authorization from the center. However, turnaround time was short, only a few days, so you could proceed quickly.

So, if an opportunity appeared—say, for example, a former high-ranking US military officer, who now is a leading figure in the disarmament movement, were to visit Japan—you could move quickly to take advantage of this target?

Yes. We would quickly make recommendations to the center, and receive Moscow's position. For such a special case, the response would be immediate.

How is the effectiveness measured of the operations carried out by the officer in the field? Is there close oversight? How important are results?

First of all, the field officer's activities are closely monitored and evaluated in fitness reports. Success is of vital importance. However, measuring success is sometimes complicated. Certain things are easy to measure and evaluate—for instance, the output of a journalist you had recruited (the number of articles published, or the amount of confidential information collected), or the parliamentary activities of one of your agents (making certain statements, initiating certain discussions, or creating a favorable atmosphere supporting Soviet goals in parliament).

These elements are evaluated against certain standards by your superiors.

Other operations, on the other hand, are more difficult to assess. For example, the success of the peace movement in Europe is a fact, and the KGB and the ID have been extensively involved. However, the growth of the European peace movement cannot be attributed solely to KGB and ID involvement. Hence, the evaluation of the effectiveness of active measures operations in the growth of the peace movement is more subjective. Still, the head of the local KGB residency and the chief of the active measures group are responsible for evaluating and rating such activities.

What happens in the case of failure?

If the individual officer fails to produce, this ultimately can lead to his being called home. However, generally the members of the active measures group will attempt to assist and advise the officer in ways of improving performance. The way to prevent failure at this level is extensive training and learning before an officer begins to conduct operations. This includes training both at home and abroad. The KGB realizes this, and the resources are available for this training. The importance of this type of investment is understood. When a major operation fails, there is an extensive review, but the failure itself will not paralyze the residency. You pick up the pieces, wait awhile, and then begin again. The current situation in Japan as a result of my defection in 1979 is an example of one such situation.

Many persons in the West discount the Soviet use of agents of influence, international front organizations, and other active measures operations as either not very important or not very effective. How would you respond to this assertion?

First of all, indicators do exist of the importance the Soviets place in these activities. The size of the overt and covert active measures effort is massive, and this can be studied and documented. I can tell you from an insider's vantage point that the ID and the KGB receive all the resources and personnel needed to carry out this massive effort. There are never any shortages. Of course, this is not a recent development. An examination of the history of the CPSU will demonstrate the importance of such tactics. A close reading of what Soviet leaders write and say also provides insight into the importance of these measures. Although we discussed effectiveness earlier, let me restate that all active measures operations are assessed against a set of standards. Success is a vital ingredient. The growth of the Soviet active measures effort over the last five to ten years is due to progress in the field.

CHAPTER VI

CONCLUSION

LEADERS IN THE KREMLIN clearly view overt and covert propaganda and political influence techniques as important means to achieve their goals. This is not surprising, in view of the origins and the mode of development of the Soviet political system. In their seizure of power, the Bolsheviks relied largely on a combination of propaganda and other political measures, together with armed force, to bring down the provisional government. Once Bolshevik power was consolidated, these techniques were institutionalized as adjuncts to traditional instruments of statecraft. They continue to be used today to influence the policies of other governments, undermine confidence in the leaders and institutions of these states, disrupt relations between various nations, and discredit and weaken major opponents.

Few studies of Soviet affairs have sought to examine how Moscow currently employs these foreign policy tools. The reasons for this oversight are not clear. A partial explanation may be found in the opinion of many specialists that since the Soviet Union has become a superpower, Kremlin leaders no longer regard propaganda and political influence operations as important. This study refutes that contention. During the 1960–1980 period, Moscow placed increasing emphasis on such traditional instruments of statecraft as diplomacy, military assistance, and economic aid. These developments, however, did not reduce or impair the Soviet program of active measures.

Examination of the years between 1960 and 1980 demonstrates that the Soviet Union devoted extensive resources to discrediting, isolating, and splitting the Western alliance through the use of propaganda and political influence activities as part of its broader political-military strategy. For these purposes, the Politburo developed a highly centralized and tightly coordinated organizational structure for planning and implementing active measures. The size of this structure and the degree of Politburo control indicate the importance Soviet leaders place in these tactics. Available evidence also suggests that the means devoted to active measures have expanded significantly during these years.

Our analysis of such overt propaganda sources as *New Times* and *Pravda*'s "International Review" also demonstrates that although the particular issues and events covered by the Soviet media have varied, Moscow's overall propaganda message basically has remained unchanged during recent decades. The major propaganda themes directed against the West consistently have sought to characterize US military and political policy as the cause of most international conflict; to demonstrate that the United States is an aggressive, militaristic, and imperial power; and to isolate Washington from its allies and friends. In sum, whether the Western allies have perceived East-West relations to be in a period of cold war or a period of "detente," Soviet overt propaganda has continued to portray the United States and NATO in negative and defamatory terms. However, the study demonstrates that at the same time, Moscow's propaganda campaign against the West has become more sophisticated, complex, and flexible.

While the United States consistently was characterized as the major threat to world peace, careful analysis of Soviet propaganda indicates that in reality the Kremlin did not perceive any direct threat or challenge to its security interests emanating from alleged US aggressiveness and militarism. The incongruity between Soviet propaganda and Moscow's actual threat perception may be explained partially by considering the tactical foreign policy objectives of the Kremlin rather than its immediate security concerns.

In other words, Moscow's primary purpose in employing foreign propaganda is not to warn the United States and its NATO allies of genuine Soviet anxiety. Rather, Soviet leaders to a great extent use this instrument as part of a political-military strategy that seeks to weaken the Western alliance. Our examination also reveals that the divisions within NATO which appeared during the latter half of the 1970s were perceived by Moscow as an attractive propaganda target, and resulted in an escalation of Soviet overt propaganda directed toward exploiting the cleavages among the Western states.

It also is clear that Moscow actively combines overt propaganda and covert political techniques. The Soviets employ a wide range of active measures to manipulate, mislead, and deceive Western targets. This study has focused on international front organizations, agents of influence, and forgeries to demonstrate how the Kremlin pursues a given policy objective through both covert and overt channels. When opposition to the modernization of NATO's intermediate-range nuclear forces became a principal theme in *Pravda* and *New Times*, for example, the Soviets quickly employed the World Peace Council and other fronts, agents such as Pierre-Charles Pathe, and forged documents to focus even more attention on the subject. Other examples of this carefully orchestrated and highly integrated approach are documented in the study.

Finally, the interviews with former Soviet bloc intelligence officers provide unique insights into the planning, implementation, and evaluation of Soviet active measures. Bittman and Levchenko reveal the high degree of control exercised by the Kremlin over active measures conducted by the KGB and the Eastern bloc intelligence services. Both are convinced that Soviet leaders view these techniques as important. They report that during the period they served as intelligence officers, Moscow continued to increase the already extensive organizational and financial resources devoted to these activities. With this expansion, Bittman and Levchenko suggest, the Kremlin gained the ability to conduct active measures on a massive, worldwide scale against the United States and NATO (as well as other targets).

Will the Soviets in the 1980s continue to employ overt and covert propaganda and political influence techniques against the United States and other members of the Western alliance? Will these activities escalate? We cannot be certain, but the answer to both questions appears to be "yes." Moscow apparently has been impressed with its own programs. As Levchenko and others point out, the growth in the size and scope of Soviet active measures campaigns can be seen as an important indicator of the degree to which the Kremlin has perceived these actions as successful. Given this conviction, it can be expected that the Soviet leadership will continue to employ and perhaps expand active measures operations against the NATO allies in the near and more distant future.

A second factor contributing to this prognosis is the central position of Yuri Andropov. During his 1967–1982 tenure as chief of the KGB, Andropov was responsible for directing the rapid growth and development of the KGB's worldwide program of covert active measures. As this study demonstrates, the KGB program was an important part of the overall Soviet effort against the West during the 1960–1980 period. It is unlikely that Andropov, as head of the entire Soviet system, will reduce or downplay the use of a policy instrument which he expanded and fine-tuned as KGB chief. Indeed, his lieutenants in the KGB and the CPSU, who were promoted for their active measures activities, are certain to provide an institutional momentum that probably will outlive Andropov's tenure as Party leader.

This is not meant to imply that the Soviet program of propaganda and political influence operations has suffered no setbacks, or that it has no weaknesses. Active measures are vulnerable to exposure. Our findings demonstrate that some of Moscow's activities indeed have been traceable. Nevertheless, the Kremlin appears willing to devote the resources it deems necessary to conduct these measures vigorously and on a worldwide basis. Furthermore, two decades of organizational growth and centralization have resulted in a more intensive, integrated, and sophisticated campaign of overt and covert techniques directed against the West. Tactical shifts in technique and the introduction of new themes undoubtedly will occur with the ebb and flow of world politics, but Moscow's strategic use of active measures is most likely to continue during the 1980s.

These developments carry important policy implications for the United States and its allies, a full examination of which is beyond the scope of this study. The Kremlin is aware of major Western vulnerabilities and the resulting opportunities for conducting active measures. Over the last twenty years, the Soviets increasingly have attempted to exploit these vulnerabilities. The NATO allies, on the other hand, until very recently have paid little attention publicly to these Soviet activities. Has this been wise? Should Western governments ignore the subject? Alternatively, should Western leaders explain to their citizens the scope, objectives, and methods of Moscow's political thrust against the United States and NATO? Should journalists, parliamentarians, and other targets of the Soviet effort be given an opportunity to learn how and why Moscow seeks to influence them? Western governments could seek to expose publicly Soviet active measures operations. Should this be done?

What other options are open to the United States and its allies? Throughout history, both in peacetime and during time of conflict, nations have included among their policy options the use of propaganda, diplomacy, and political action to influence attitudes and behavior in foreign lands. When a state is faced with an adversary willing to devote massive resources to carefully orchestrated campaigns of overt and covert political warfare, unilateral restraint and failure to use a comparable variety of available instruments could lead to serious political and security setbacks.

This does not mean that the United States and its allies should merely react to Soviet initiatives. Nor should the United States undertake to employ each and every one of the techniques used by the Kremlin. Rather, Western methods of political action, consistent with Western values, should be utilized. Some forms of action might be designed specifically to counter Soviet active measures. Others should be employed no matter what Moscow does. In other words, Western political action should be designed not only to counter Soviet efforts, but to promote actively the principles and objectives of democracy.

Proposals of this sort often become quite controversial. During the last years of the Carter Administration and during the Reagan Administration, however, there has been growing recognition in Washington of the importance not only of countering Moscow's campaigns but also of assisting democratic forces. The creation of an intergovernmental coordinating mechanism for what is now called "public diplomacy" through National Security Decision Directive 77, and the establishment of the National Endowment for Democracy, designed to promote democracy abroad, are tangible indications of Washington's general direction in the early 1980s.

At this juncture, it is not possible to say with any degree of assurance that the United States and the NATO governments will effectively sustain such initiatives. Nor can we know the extent to which non-governmental organizations in these states and the Western media will support or impede this policy direction. Affirmative answers to such questions are needed. Without such affirmation, it is far from clear that the West is prepared to meet the almost-certain challenge of Soviet active measures in the 1980s.

GLOSSARY

Active Measures

A Soviet term that came into use in the 1950s to describe certain overt and covert techniques for influencing events and behavior in, and the actions of, foreign countries. Active measures may entail influencing the policies of another government, undermining confidence in its leaders and institutions, disrupting relations between other nations, and discrediting and weakening governmental and non-governmental opponents. This frequently involves attempts to deceive the target (foreign governmental and non-governmental elites or mass audiences), and to distort the target's perceptions of reality.

Active measures may be conducted overtly through officially-sponsored foreign propaganda channels, diplomatic relations, and cultural diplomacy. Covert political techniques include the use of covert propaganda, oral and written disinformation, agents of influence, clandestine radios, and international front organizations. Although active measures principally are political in nature, military maneuvers and paramilitary assistance to insurgents and terrorists also may be involved.

Agent of Influence

An agent of influence is a person who uses his or her position, influence, power, and credibility to promote the objectives of a foreign power in ways unattributable to that power. Influence operations may be carried out by controlled agents (persons who are recruited, and advance the interests of a foreign power in response to specific orders); "trusted contacts" (persons who consciously collaborate to advance the objectives of a foreign power, but who are not formally recruited and controlled); and unwitting but manipulated individuals.

Correlation of Forces

The Soviet term "correlation of forces" refers to the assessment of world power. It is broader and more complex than the traditional Western concept of "balance of power," and takes into account contradictions in the enemy camp and many intangible as well as tangible elements of power. In addition to military factors, this assessment includes economic components, and estimates of national and international social, political, and revolutionary trends. In Soviet doctrine, policy priorities and offensive and defensive strategy at any given stage of history are to flow from a determination of the correlation of forces.

Covert Propaganda

Propaganda is defined as written or oral information which deliberately seeks to influence and/or manipulate the opinions and attitudes of a given target audience. In the case of covert propaganda, the communication emanates from a falsely attributed or non-attributed source, and is disseminated through various media channels. These include campaigns orchestrated in the world press by journalists acting as agents of influence clandestine radio broadcasts, and the propaganda activities of international front organizations.

Disinformation (Conducted Covertly)

Disinformation may be either overt or covert. This study is concerned only with disinformation operations that are conducted secretly. Covert disinformation is non-attributed or falsely attributed communication, written or oral, containing intentionally false, incomplete, or misleading information (frequently combined with true information), which seeks to deceive, misinform, and/or mislead the target. Either foreign governmental and nongovernmental elites, or a foreign mass audience, may comprise the target.

The objective of disinformation is to lead the target to believe in the veracity of the message and consequently to act in the interests of the nation conducting the disinformation operation. This technique may be advanced through rumors, forgeries, manipulative political actions, agents of influence, front organizations, and other means. Until the 1950s, the term *dezinformatsia* was used in some Soviet circles to refer to what Soviet leaders now call "active measures." *Dezinformatsia* currently is used in Moscow to refer to a specific type of active measures technique, here called "disinformation."

Forgery

Forgery, one of many disinformation techniques, is the use of authentic-looking but false documents and communiqués. The falsified documents examined in this study include altered or distorted versions of actual US government documents obtained by the Soviets (usually through espionage), and the documents which have been entirely fabricated. The principal targets of forgeries tend to be foreign governmental or non-governmental elites, although mass audiences also can be targeted.

International Department, CPSU

Established in the mid-1950s, the International Department (ID) and the CPSU Central Committee reportedly is responsible for (a) foreign policy planning concerning non-Communist governments and non-governmental organizations, and (b) planning, coordinating, and conducting active measures. The latter function includes administering, funding, and coordinating the activities of well over a dozen international front organizations. The ID also carries out active measures through its liaison with non-ruling Communist parties and revolutionary movements and the non-governmental organizations they control. Through international meetings, representatives stationed abroad, and the monthly journal *Problems of Peace and Socialism* (known in its English-language edition as *World Marxist Review*), the ID communicates official instructions and guidelines to foreign Communist parties, insurgent movements, and front organizations.

International Front Organizations

While purporting to be independent non-governmental organizations, in reality international front organizations are established and directed by the CPSU to promote its foreign policy objectives. Tactics utilized by a front organization may include propaganda and political influence operations. Since the mid-1950s, Soviet international fronts have been directed by the International Department (ID) of the CPSU. Among the leading Soviet fronts are the World Peace Council (WPC), the World Federation Trade Unions (WFTU), the World Federation of Democratic Youth (WFDY), and the International Union of Students (IUS).

International Information Department, CPSU

The International Information Department (IID) of the CPSU Central Committee apparently was established in 1978. There is conflicting evidence regarding the purpose of this department and the scope of its responsibilities. Some Western analysts believe it was created to improve the Soviet foreign propaganda effort through more centralized and efficient integration of the wide range of outlets employed. Other evidence suggests that the IID neither sets the propaganda line for foreign communication channels nor has responsibility for their programmatic guidance. In this regard, it appears that the IID is less significant than the ID.

Overt Propaganda

Overt propaganda is written or oral information from an unconcealed government source which deliberately seeks to influence and/or manipulate the opinions and attitudes of other persons. A government may direct its propaganda toward either a domestic or a foreign mass audience. Propaganda does not necessarily reflect concern with accuracy or truthfulness. Soviet overt propaganda increasingly has been characterized by intensity and concentration; flexibility and adaptability; and centralized control and coordination.

Political Warfare

Broadly defined, political warfare is the threat to employ or the actual use of overt and covert political, economic, and military techniques to influence politics and events in foreign countries. The objective is to persuade the target to behave in ways that are directly or indirectly supportive of the nation conducting the political warfare. During the twentieth century, various governments have defined and employed political warfare in different ways, depending in large part on the type of regime involved and the particular situation at hand.

Service A of the KGB's First Chief Directorate

Service A, located within the KGB's First Chief Directorate, has responsibility for planning and conducting covert active measures. These include agent-of-influence operations, oral and written disinformation, forgeries, and other types of covert political action.

NOTES

CHAPTER 1

1. William Griffith, "Bonn and Washington: From Deterioration to Crisis?", *Orbis* (Spring 1982), pp. 122–123.
2. In the early 1980s, articles began to appear focusing on the relationship between the Soviet Union and the European peace movement. See Vladimir Bukovsky, "The Peace Movement and the Soviet Union," *Commentary* (May 1982), pp. 1–36; Wynfred Joshua, "Soviet Manipulation of the European Peace Movement," *Strategic Review* (Winter 1983), pp. 9–18; and J. A. Emerson Vermaat, "Moscow Fronts and the European Peace Movement," *Problems of Communism* (November–December 1982), pp. 43–56. See also John Barron, *The KGB Today: The Hidden Hand* (New York: Reader's Digest Press, 1983).

CHAPTER 2

1. Joseph L. Nogee and Robert H. Donaldson, *Soviet Foreign Policy Since World War II* (New York: Pergamon Press, 1981), pp. 33–34. See also Nathan C. Leites, *A Study of Bolshevism* (Glencoe, IL: Free Press, 1953).
2. Adam Ulam, "The Soviet Union and the Rules of the International Game," in Kurt London, ed., *The Soviet Union in World Politics* (Boulder, CO: Westview, 1980), pp. 48–49.

3. We recommend the following important theoretical treatments: Leonid Brezhnev, *Selected Speeches and Writings on Foreign Affairs* (New York: Pergamon Press, 1979); Mikhail Suslov, *Selected Speeches and Writings* (New York: Pergamon Press, 1982); Boris Ponomarev, "Invincibility of the Liberation Movement," *Kommunist*, No. 1 (1980), pp. 11–27, translated in *FBIS Daily Report*, Soviet Union, Vol. 3, No. 24 (February 4, 1980); and V. V. Zagladin, ed., *The World Communist Movement* (Moscow: Progress Publishers, 1973).

   Useful insights also can be drawn from *25th Congress of the Communist Party of the Soviet Union, Documents and Resolutions* (Moscow: Novosti, 1976). These views also are strongly expressed in Soviet military writings. See especially the recent compilation edited by Harriet Fast Scott and William F. Scott entitled *The Soviet Art of War: Doctrine, Strategy, and Tactics* (Boulder, CO: Westview, 1982).

4. *Pravda*, October 19, 1973, cited in *Current Digest of the Soviet Press*, Vol. 25, No. 43 (November 21, 1973), p. 6.

5. *Pravda*, February 25, 1976, cited in *Current Digest of the Soviet Press*, Vol. 28, No. 8 (March 24, 1976), p. 14.

6. Marshal A. A. Grechko, *The Armed Forces of the Soviet State*, US Air Force translation (Washington, DC: GPO, 1975). Chapter One contains a detailed discussion of Lenin's views on war and the armed forces, and the continuing relevance of Lenin today.

7. N. Inozemtsev, "Problems of Modern World Development and International Relations," *Kommunist* (October 1976), p. 78.

8. R. Judson Mitchell, *Ideology of a Superpower: Contemporary Soviet Doctrine on International Relations* (Stanford: Hoover Institution Press, 1982), Chapter 5.

   See also Nogee and Donaldson, *Soviet Foreign Policy Since World War II*; Alvin Rubinstein, *Soviet Foreign Policy Since World War II: Imperial and Global* (Cambridge, MA: Winthrop Publishers, 1981); Adam Ulam, *Expansion and Coexistence: Soviet Foreign Policy, 1917–73* (New York: Praeger, 1974); Erik Hoffman and Frederic Fleron, ed., *The Conduct of Soviet Foreign Policy* (Chicago: Aldine Publishing Co., 1980); Morton Schwartz, *The Foreign Policy of the USSR* (Encino, CA: Dickenson Publishing Co., 1976); Vernon Aspaturian, *Process and Power in Soviet Foreign Policy* (Boston: Little, Brown, 1971); and Alain Besancon, *The Soviet Syndrome* (New York: Harcourt, Brace, Jovanovich, 1978).

9. These factors include the external environment, threats posed by potential enemies, opportunities that arise unexpectedly, domestic conditions, the political security of the leadership, economic conditions, and so on—in other words, the general factors that basic texts identify as the key influences on state behavior. For classic statements see Hans Morgenthau, *Politics Among Nations*, 5th ed. (New York: Alfred A. Knopf, 1973); and Kenneth Waltz, *Man, the State, and War* (New York: Columbia University Press, 1965).

10. Rubinstein, *Soviet Foreign Policy Since World War II: Imperial and Global*, pp. 269–271.

11. Relatively recent works by Rubinstein, Ulam, Nogee and Donaldson, Schwartz, and Mitchell have been cited in previous notes. The most important earlier studies include Louis Fischer, *The Soviets in World Affairs*, 2 vols. (New York: Vintage Books, 1960); Max Beloff, *The Foreign Policy of Soviet Russia, 1929–1941*, 2 vols. (London: Oxford University Press, 1947–1955); George Kennan, *Russia and the West Under Lenin and Stalin* (Boston: Little, Brown, 1961); Philip Mosely, *The Kremlin and World Politics* (New York: Vintage Books, 1960); Hugh Seton-Watson, *From Lenin to Khrushchev* (New York: Praeger, 1960); and Robert Wesson, *Soviet Foreign Policy in Perspective* (Homewood, IL: Dorsey, 1969).

12. Important current assessments of Soviet military strategy include Harriet Fast Scott and William F. Scott, *The Armed Forces of the USSR* (Boulder, CO: Westview, 1979); Derek Leebaert, ed., *Soviet Military Thinking* (London: George Allen and Unwin, 1981); Ken Booth, *The Military Instrument in Soviet Foreign Policy, 1917–1972* (London: Royal United Services Institute, 1973); Joseph D. Douglass, Jr. and Amoretta H. Hoeber, *Soviet Strategy for Nuclear War* (Stanford: Hoover Institution Press, 1979); Joseph D. Douglass, Jr., *Soviet Military Strategy in Europe* (New York: Pergamon Press, 1980); John Erickson, *Soviet Military Power* (London: Royal United Services Institute, 1971); and John Dziak, *Soviet Perceptions of Military Power: The Interaction of Theory and Practice* (New York: Crane, Russak and Co., 1981).

    While much has been written on Soviet military strategy and how it may serve political purposes, there exists no comprehensive, current study of the political warfare side of Soviet strategy. For a discussion of this subject, one must look to studies published in the 1950s and the 1960s. An example is Robert Strausz-Hupe, et al., *Protracted Conflict* (New York: Harper, 1959).

13. Michael Deane, "The Soviet Assessment of the Correlation of Forces: Implications for American Foreign Policy," *Orbis* (Fall 1976), p. 627.

14. While the literature on the balance of power is extensive, until recently little had been written on the manner in which the Soviets assess the world balance of forces, or "correlation of forces." Works such as Mitchell's *Ideology of a Superpower* are breaking new ground in this area.

15. Vernon Aspaturian, "Soviet Global Power and the Correlation of Forces," *Problems of Communism* (May-June 1980), p. 8.

16. This is not to say that Western analysts always fail to consider other factors. However, an examination of the work of Morgenthau, Inis Claude, Klaus Knorr, and other leading writers on the balance of power will demonstrate the dominance of military and economic factors in this assessment. See Morgenthau, *Politics Among Nations*; Claude, *Power*

and International Relations (New York: Random House, 1962); and Knorr, *The Power of Nations* (New York: Basic Books, 1975).

17. G. Shakhazarov, "On the Problems of the Correlation of Forces," *Kommunist*, No. 3 (February 1974); and S. Sanakoyev, "The World Today: Problems of the Correlation of Forces," *International Affairs* (November 1974).

18. Serjiyen, "Leninism on the Correlation of Forces as a Factor of International Relations," *International Affairs* (May 1975), p. 103.

19. V. Kortunov, "The Leninist Policy of Peaceful Co-Existence and Class Struggle," *International Affairs* (May 1979); and N. Kapchenko, "Leninist Foreign Policy: A Transformative Force," *International Affairs* (October 1978).

20. On this point Mitchell explains that the Soviets have maintained a "traditional preference for avoiding frontal conflict with the principal enemy and for the achievement of ends by flanking maneuvers and concentration on the fringes rather than the center of the opposing system." *Ideology of a Superpower*, p. 57. While Mitchell is correct, it also is the case, as the present study demonstrates, that the Soviets employ political warfare measures directly against the center of the major opposing system.

21. During the 1970s, there was extensive Soviet commentary on this subject. For authoritative discussion by the Soviets on this issue, see the documents from the 24th and 25th Party Congresses. *24th Congress of the Communist Party of the Soviet Union, March 30-April 9, 1971, Documents* (Moscow: Novosti, 1971); and *25th Congress of the Communist Party of the Soviet Union, Documents and Resolutions*. For analyses of this Soviet commentary by Western specialists on Soviet foreign policy, see Mitchell, *Ideology of a Superpower*, Chapters 5, 6, 8, and 9; Rubinstein, *Soviet Foreign Policy Since World War II*, Chapter 12; and London, ed., *The Soviet Union in World Politics*, Chapter 13.

22. Speech by Leonid Brezhnev, *Pravda*, October 15, 1975, p. 1. Translated in *Current Digest of the Soviet Press*, Vol. 27, No. 42 (1975), p. 13. For an excellent analysis of Soviet views on detente and peaceful coexistence, see *Research Notes on US-Soviet Affairs*, No. 1 (July 1978), edited by Mose Harvey and Foy Kohler of the Center for Advanced International Studies.

23. Sun Tzu, *The Art of War* (London: Oxford University Press, 1963), pp. 144–149.

24. On the classical Indian arthasastra system and its historical evolution, see Chanakya, *Kautilya's Arthasastra*, 4th ed., R. Shamasastry, et al., trans. (Mysore: Sri Raghuveer Printing Press, 1951); John Spellman, *Political Theory of Ancient India* (Oxford: Clarendon Press, 1964); and K. M. Panikkar, *A Survey of Indian History* (Bombay: Asia Publishing House, 1957).

25. For a fascinating discussion see Adda Bozeman, "Covert Action and

Foreign Policy," in Roy Godson, ed., *Intelligence Requirements for the 1980s: Covert Action* (New York: National Strategy Information Center, 1981), pp. 15–78. For an interesting treatment of the use of psychological warfare throughout history see Paul Linebarger, *Psychological Warfare* (Washington, DC: Infantry Journal Press, 1948), Chapter 1.

26. For a useful overview of the Nazi and Soviet approaches, see Andrew Scott, *The Revolution in Statecraft: Informal Penetration* (New York: Random House, 1965), Chapter 2. The Nazi experience will not be examined in the present study. Readers interested in a fuller treatment than is offered by Scott should see Louis de Jong, *The German Fifth Column in the Second World War* (London: Routledge, 1956); Z. A. B. Zeman, *Nazi Propaganda*, 2nd ed. (New York: Oxford University Press, 1973); and Louis Lochner, *The Goebbels Diaries* (New York: Doubleday, 1948).

27. For an informed discussion of these developments by a group of former senior intelligence officers and knowledgeable experts, see Godson, ed., *Intelligence Requirements for the 1980s: Covert Action.*

28. For an interesting discussion of how these concepts were used interchangeably, see Roland Perusse, "Psychological Warfare Reappraised," in William Daugherty and Morris Janowitz, ed., *A Psychological Warfare Casebook* (Baltimore: John Hopkins University Press, 1958), pp. 25–26.

    Selected scholarly research and writing on psychological warfare from the 1950s to the early 1960s includes Linebarger, *Psychological Warfare*; Daugherty and Janowitz, ed., *A Psychological Warfare Casebook*; Daniel Lerner, ed., *Propaganda in War and Crisis* (New York: Stewart Publishers, 1950); Leonard Doob, *Public Opinion and Propaganda* (New York: Holt and Co., 1948); Jacques Ellul, *Propaganda: The Formation of Men's Attitudes* (New York: Alfred A. Knopf, 1965); W. Phillips Davison, *International Political Communication* (New York: Praeger, 1965); and Harold Lasswell, Nathan Leites, and associates, *Language of Politics: Studies in Quantitative Semantics* (New York: Stewart Publishers, 1949).

29. William Daugherty, "Changing Concepts," in Daugherty and Janowitz, ed., *A Psychological Warfare Casebook*, pp. 12–18.

30. Harold Lasswell, "Political and Psychological Warfare," in Daugherty and Janowitz, ed., *A Psychological Warfare Casebook*, p. 24. Linebarger also presents a relatively inclusive definition: "Political warfare consists of the framing of the national policy in such a way as to assist propaganda or military operations, whether with respect to direct political relations of government with one another or in relation to groups of people possessing political character." *Psychological Warfare*, p. 47.

31. In an examination of the scholarly literature on international relations, one is hard-pressed to find texts that approach overt and covert mea-

sures in an integrated fashion. Writers in the 1950s and the 1960s treated these measures as important but separate tools of statecraft. In the 1970s, many newer texts failed to include sections on propaganda and covert action, revealing the perception that these two measures are not important. A recent important exception is K. J. Holsti, *International Politics: A Framework for Analysis*, 4th ed. (Englewood Cliffs, NJ: Prentice-Hall, 1983).

32. See Godson, ed., *Intelligence Requirements for the 1980s: Covert Action*, pp. 1–11 and 193–207.

33. Angelo Codevilla, "Covert Action and Foreign Policy," in Godson, ed., *Intelligence Requirements for the 1980s: Covert Action*, p. 79.

34. For commentary on Nazi tactics, see previously cited works, particularly Ellul, *Propaganda*.

35. For example, see Alfred Meyer, *Leninism* (Cambridge, MA: Harvard University Press, 1957); Bertram Wolfe, *An Ideology in Power* (New York: Stein and Day, 1969); Leonard Schapiro, *The Communist Party of the Soviet Union*, rev. ed. (New York: Random House, 1971); Adam Ulam, *The Bolsheviks* (New York: Macmillan, 1965); and Merle Fainsod, *How Russia is Ruled*, rev. ed. (Cambridge, MA: Harvard University Press, 1963).

36. Bertram Wolfe, *Three Who Made a Revolution*, rev. ed. (New York: Delta, 1964); E. H. Carr, *A History of Soviet Russia*, 3 vols. (New York: Macmillan, 1950, 1951, 1952); and Ulam, *The Bolsheviks*.

37. Leonard Schapiro, "Totalitarianism in Foreign Policy," in London, ed., *The Soviet Union in World Politics*, pp. 8–9.

38. Information on the history and development of these tactics of political warfare can be deduced from the following materials: literature on the history of the CPSU; materials on the Comintern; literature on the Soviet intelligence services; and first-hand accounts by persons who practiced active measures before defecting from the USSR. For the latter two categories, the present authors made extensive use of the *Bibliography on the Soviet Intelligence and Security Services* (New York: National Strategy Information Center, [1984]). This bibliography contains over 400 annotated sources.

39. For an interesting, first-hand account by a former KGB officer who specialized in these techniques, see Alexander Kaznacheyev, *Inside a Soviet Embassy: Experiences of a Russian Diplomat in Burma* (New York: Ballantine, 1981).

40. Frederick Barghoorn, *Politics in the USSR*, 2nd ed. (Boston: Little, Brown, 1972); Schapiro, *The Communist Party of the Soviet Union*; Robert Conquest, *Power and Policy in the USSR* (New York: Harper and Row, 1967); Fainsod, *How Russia is Ruled*; John Reshetar, *The Soviet Polity*, 2nd ed. (New York: Harper and Row, 1978); and John Armstrong, *Ideology, Politics and Government in the Soviet Union*, 4th ed. (New York: Praeger, 1978).

41. Reshetar, *The Soviet Polity*, p. 125.

42. Armstrong, *Ideology, Politics, and Government in the Soviet Union*, pp. 81–82. See also Conquest, *Power and Policy in the USSR*; and Carl Linden, *Khrushchev and the Soviet Leadership, 1957–1964* (Baltimore: Johns Hopkins University Press, 1966).

43. For the classic discussion of this point see Philip Selznick, *The Organizational Weapon: A Study of Bolshevik Strategy and Tactics* (New York: McGraw-Hill, 1952). Lenin's perspective on this subject is presented in V. I. Lenin, *What Is To Be Done?* (New York: International Publishers, 1969).

44. Wilbur Schramm, "Soviet Concept of Psychological Warfare," in Daugherty and Janowitz, ed., *A Psychological Warfare Casebook*, pp. 782–783.

45. Among the best general works on the Comintern are Gunther Nollau, *International Communism and World Revolution, History and Methods* (London: Hollis and Carter, 1961); and Franz Borkenau, *World Communism* (Ann Arbor, MI: University of Michigan Press, 1962).

46. Leonard Schapiro, "The International Department of the CPSU: Key to Soviet Policy," *International Journal* (Winter 1976–1977), p. 42.

47. *Ibid.*

48. "The Foreign Departments of the Central Committee of the CPSU," *Radio Liberty Research Bulletin* (October 27, 1980), pp. 13–14.

49. Report of a Study Group of the Institute for Conflict Studies, *The Strategic Intentions of the Soviet Union* (London: Institute for Conflict Studies, 1978), pp. 13–14.

50. Schapiro, "The International Department of the CPSU: Key to Soviet Policy," p. 44. Schapiro even notes that the ID gained responsibility for appointments within the Foreign Service.

51. *Ibid.*, pp. 43–44. For an interesting discussion of these "think tanks," see Richard Soll, Arthur Zuehlke, and Richard Foster, *The Role of Social Science Research Institutes in the Formulation and Execution of Soviet Foreign Policy* (Arlington, VA: SRI International, 1976). For a somewhat different perspective, see Morton Schwartz, *Soviet Perceptions of the United States* (Los Angeles: University of California Press, 1974).

52. See Cord Meyer, *Facing Reality* (New York: Harper and Row, 1980), Chapters 13 and 14.

53. The most complete annual listing of these various groups can be found in Richard Staar, ed., *Yearbook on International Communist Affairs* (Stanford: Hoover Institution Press). This yearbook has been published annually since 1966.

54. Most of the post-World War II literature on the Soviet use of international fronts was published in the 1950s and the early 1960s. For example, the periodical *Problems of Communism* gave wide coverage to these developments in such articles as Robert Boss, "Communist

Fronts: Their History and Function," *Problems of Communism* (September-October 1960); Otto Pick and Andrew Wiseman, "Moscow and the WFTU," *Problems of Communism* (May-June 1959); and Morton Schwartz, "Moscow's Experimental Venture: The Vienna World Youth Festival," *Problems of Communism* (July-August 1959). This earlier period also produced a number of scholarly books on the subject. See Jeane Kirkpatrick, ed., *The Strategy of Deception* (New York: Farrar, Straus, and Co., 1963); Frederick Barghoorn, *The Soviet Cultural Offensive* (Princeton: Princeton University Press, 1960); and James Atkinson, *The Politics of Struggle: The Communist Front and Political Warfare* (Chicago: Henry Regnery Co., 1966).

By the 1970s, Soviet fronts were receiving much less attention in the scholarly literature. One exception is Roy Godson, *The Kremlin and Labor* (New York: Crane, Russak and Co., 1977). (Godson published new study, *Labor in Soviet Global Strategy*, in 1984.)

55. Other examples of clandestine radios operated by the Soviets include Radio Bha Yi, or 1st August Radio, directed at China; Our Radio (Vizim Radio) and the Voice of the Communist Party of Turkey (VCPT) aimed at Turkey; and the Voice of Truth aimed at Greece.

56. For a background sketch of Ponomarev, see Reshetar, *The Soviet Polity*, p. 147; and "The Foreign Departments of the Central Committee of the CPSU," *Radio Liberty Research Bulletin*, pp. 14–18 and 21–24.

57. For a useful review of Ponomarev's writing, see "The Foreign Departments of the CPSU," pp. 14–24. See also Mitchell's commentary on Ponomarev in *Ideology of a Superpower*, pp. 75–87 and 123–124.

58. Frederick Barghoorn, *Soviet Foreign Propaganda* (Princeton: Princeton University Press, 1964), pp. 244–250. On the historical development of the Department of Propaganda and Agitation, see Herbert McCloskey and John Turner, *The Soviet Dictatorship* (New York: McGraw-Hill, 1960).

59. See Robert Conquest, ed., *The Politics of Ideas in the USSR* (London: Bodley Head, 1967); Schapiro, *The Communist Party of the Soviet Union*; Mark Hopkins, *Mass Media in the Soviet Union* (New York: Pegasus, 1970); and *External Information and Cultural Relations Programs of the Union of Soviet Socialist Republics* (Washington, DC: USIA Office of Research Assessment, 1973).

60. Reshetar, *The Soviet Polity*, p. 147.

61. Identified in *Pravda*, December 12, 1965. Cited in "The Foreign Departments of the Central Committee of the CPSU," p. 18.

62. Because the IID is such a new department, little has been written about it. Useful exceptions include "The International Information Department of the Central Committee of the CPSU," *Radio Liberty Research Report* (March 4, 1980); and US Congress, House, Permanent Select Committee on Intelligence, "Soviet Active Measures," 97th Congress, 2nd Session (Washington, DC: GPO, 1982).

63. *FBIS Daily Report*, Soviet Union, Vol. III (June 15, 1983), p. R15.

64. See Barghoorn, *Soviet Foreign Propaganda*; John Clews, *Communist Propaganda Techniques* (New York: Praeger, 1964); Davison, *International Political Communication*; Ellul, *Propaganda*; and Alex Inkeles, *Social Changes in Soviet Russia* (Cambridge, MA: Harvard University Press, 1968).

65. Figures are drawn from *External Information and Cultural Relations Programs of the Union of Soviet Socialist Republics*, p. 127; *Soviet External Radio Broadcasts, 1970–1978* (Washington, DC: USIA Office of Research, 1979), p. III; and *Communist International Radio Broadcasting in 1980* (Washington, DC: USIA Office of Research), p. 4.

66. See "Moscow's Radio Peace and Progress," in the US Department of State publication *Foreign Affairs Notes* (August 1982).

67. The Board For International Broadcasting, *1983 Annual Report* (Washington, DC: Board For International Broadcasting, 1983), p. 2.

68. *External Cultural and Information Activities and Themes of Communist Countries in 1977* (Washington, DC: USIA Office of Research, 1978), pp. 1–6.

69. *External Information and Cultural Relations Programs of the Union of Soviet Socialist Republics*, pp. 36–37.

70. *Ibid*.

71. For example, see William Lee, *Understanding the Soviet Military Threat* (New York: National Strategy Information Center, 1977).

72. Stanley Leinwoll, "Jamming—Past, Present, Future," in J. M. Frost, ed., *World Radio and TV Handbook* (Denmark: Billboard, 1982), p. 40.

73. US Congress, House, Permanent Select Committee on Intelligence, "Soviet Covert Action (The Forgery Offensive)," 96th Congress, 2nd Session (Washington, DC: GPO, 1980), p. 60.

74. US Congress, House, Permanent Select Committee on Intelligence, "Soviet Active Measures," p. 30.

75. On the subject of the Cheka, see George Leggett, *The Cheka: Lenin's Political Police* (New York: Oxford University Press, 1981).

76. See John Barron, *The KGB: The Secret Work of Soviet Secret Agents* (New York: Reader's Digest Press, 1974), and *The KGB Today: The Hidden Hand* (New York: Reader's Digest Press, 1983); David Dallin, *Soviet Espionage* (New Haven, CT: Yale University Press, 1955); Ronald Hingley, *The Russian Secret Police: Muscovite, Imperial Russian, and Soviet Political Security Operations* (New York: Simon and Schuster, 1970); Leggett, *The Cheka: Lenin's Political Police*; and Simon Wolin and Robert Slusser, ed., *The Soviet Secret Police* (New York: Praeger, 1957).

77. John Dziak, "Soviet Intelligence and Security Services in the 1980s: The Paramilitary Dimension," in Roy Godson, ed., *Intelligence*

Requirements for the 1980s: Counterintelligence (New York: National Strategy Information Center, 1980), pp. 95–113. See also Stephen T. Hosmer and Thomas W. Wolfe, *Soviet Policy and Practice Toward Third World Conflicts* (Lexington, MA: Lexington Books, 1983).

78. *Congressional Record—House* (September 28, 1965), pp. 25391–25393.

79. Barron, *The KGB*, Chapter 2; Ladislav Bittman, "Soviet Bloc 'Disinformation' and other 'Active Measures,'" in Robert L. Pfaltzgraff, Uri Ra'anan, and Warren Milberg, ed., *Intelligence Policy and National Security* (Hamden, CT: Archon Books, 1981), pp. 212–214.

80. Ladislav Bittman, *The Deception Game* (Syracuse, NY: Syracuse University Research Corp., 1972).

81. Wolfe, *Three Who Made a Revolution*, pp. 54–59. For Lenin's views on the use of the press, see *What Is To Be Done?*

82. Barghoorn, *Soviet Foreign Propaganda*, pp. 4–5.

83. In this connection, see W. Phillips Davison, "Some Trends in International Propaganda," *Annals of the American Academy of Political and Social Science* (November 1971), pp. 1–13; Gerhard Wettig, *Broadcasting and Detente* (New York: St. Martin's Press, 1977); and *External Information and Cultural Relations Programs*.

84. Barghoorn, *Soviet Foreign Propaganda*, pp. 40 and 42.

85. There is a growing literature on the role of deception in Soviet strategy. However, this literature is focused primarily on military matters. For a broader discussion of the role of deception in Soviet policy, see Ronald Hingley, *The Russian Mind* (New York: Charles Scribner's Sons, 1972), Chapter 2. With respect to military strategy and operations, see Jiri Valenta, "Soviet Use of Surprise and Deception," *Survival* (March/April 1982).

86. Barghoorn, *The Soviet Cultural Offensive*; Sylvia Marguilies, *The Pilgrimage to Russia* (Madison, WI: University of Wisconsin Press, 1968); and Paul Hollander, *Political Pilgrims: Travels of Western Intellectuals to the Soviet Union, China, and Cuba, 1928–1978* (New York: Oxford University Press, 1981).

87. "Disinformation: War With Words," *Air Force Magazine* (March 1982), pp. 85–86.

88. Cited in US Congress, House, Permanent Select Committee on Intelligence, "Soviet Covert Action (The Forgery Offensive)," p. 63.

89. Bittman, "Soviet Bloc 'Disinformation' and other 'Active Measures,'" p. 219.

90. The relevant literature usually subdivides propaganda into the following categories: white (an overt operation—the sponsor is acknowledged); gray (a covert operation—the true source is concealed and no source is given); black (a covert operation—the propaganda purports to emanate from a source other than the true one). For the purpose of this study, we find the overt-covert distinction, rather than the white-gray-

black categorization, more appropriate.

91. This early literature is quite extensive. The key works include Barghoorn, *Soviet Foreign Propaganda*; Clews, *Communist Propaganda Techniques*; Davison, *International Political Communication*; Ellul, *Propaganda*; Michael Gehlen, *The Politics of Coexistence: Soviet Methods and Motives* (Bloomington, IN: Indiana University Press, 1967); and Inkeles, *Social Change in Soviet Russia*.

CHAPTER 3

. The literature on Soviet foreign propaganda from the 1950s and the early 1960s appears to substantiate this proposition. Among the key studies, see Frederick Barghoorn, *Soviet Foreign Propaganda* (Princeton: Princeton University Press, 1964); John Clews, *Communist Propaganda Techniques* (New York: Praeger, 1964); Bowen Evans, *Worldwide Communist Propaganda Activities* (New York: Macmillan, 1955); and Evron M. Kirkpatrick, ed., *Target: The World* (New York: Macmillan, 1956).

. See Barghoorn, *Soviet Foreign Propaganda*; Clews, *Communist Propaganda Techniques*; W. Phillips Davison, *International Political Propaganda* (New York: Praeger, 1965); and Suzanne Labin, *The Technique of Soviet Propaganda* (Washington, DC: GPO, 1967).

. See William Daugherty and Morris Janowitz, ed., *A Psychological Warfare Casebook* (Baltimore: Johns Hopkins University Press, 1958); Paul Linebarger, *Psychological Warfare* (Washington, DC: Infantry Journal Press, 1948); and Daniel Lerner, ed., *Propaganda in War and Crisis* (New York: Stewart Publishers, 1950).

. Within the field of international relations, the following works constitute major contributions to the literature on this subject: Harold Lasswell, Nathan Leites, and associates, *Language of Politics: Studies in Quantitative Sermantics* (Cambridge, MA: Stewart Publishers, 1949); Ole Holsti, Robert North, and Richard Brody, "Perception and Action in the 1914 Crisis," in J. David Singer, ed., *Quantitative International Politics* (New York: Free Press, 1968); Ole Holsti, *Crisis, Escalation, War* (Montreal: McGill-Queen's University Press, 1972); Charles Hermann, et al., *Code Manual for Analytic Deck of Comparative Foreign Policy Events* (Columbus, OH: Ohio State University, 1971); Maurice A. East, "Size of Foreign Policy Behavior: A Test of Two Models," *World Politics* (July 1973), pp. 556–576; Alexander George, "The Operational Code: A Neglected Approach to the Study of Political Leaders and Decision-Making," *International Studies Quarterly* (June 1969), pp. 190–222; and Stephen Walker, "The Interface Between Beliefs and

Behavior," *Journal of Conflict Resolution* (March 1977), pp. 129–173.

Soviet communications also have been systematically analyzed. Important works include Harold Holder, "Russian Propaganda in Exchange Publications," *Journalism Quarterly* (Autumn 1965); Lasswell, Leites, and associates, *Language of Politics*; Natalie Grant, *Communist Psychological Offensive: Distortions in the Translation of Official Documents* (Washington, DC: Research Institute of the Sino-Soviet Bloc, 1961); M. C. Lodge, *Soviet Elite Attitudes Since Stalin* (Columbus, OH: Charles E. Merrill, 1969); and William Zimmerman and Robert Axelrod, "The 'Lessons' of Vietnam and Soviet Foreign Policy," *World Politics* (October 1981) and "The Soviet Press and Soviet Foreign Policy: A Usually Reliable Source," *British Journal of Political Science* (April 1981).

5. The following research questions were synthesized from the social science literature focused on the analysis of mass communications data. These questions address the kinds of issues that might guide research projects concerned with foreign propaganda analysis. (1) What are the broad trends in the communications content? (2) What differences exist in the content of the various communication channels of a particular nation? (3) How closely does government foreign propaganda content coincide with policy objectives? (4) How do one or more governments utilize different propaganda techniques? (5) What are the underlying intentions or goals of the foreign communications? (6) How effective has the foreign propaganda been in achieving its objectives? (7) How can a target government counter a foreign propaganda campaign directed against it?

These are only the most obvious research questions that might be addressed. For a broader discussion of these and related issues, see Claire Selltiz, Lawrence Wrightsman, and Stuart Cook, *Research Methods in Social Relations*, 3rd ed. (New York: Holt, Rinehart, and Winston, 1976).

6. B. Berilson, *Content Analysis in Communications Research* (Glencoe, IL: Free Press, 1952); George Gerbner, et al., ed., *The Analysis of Communications Content: Developments in Scientific Theories and Computer Techniques* (New York: Wiley, 1969); B. L. Simeth, Harold Lasswell, and R. D. Casey, *Propaganda, Communications, and Public Opinion* (Princeton: Princeton University Press, 1969); Ole Holsti, G. Aninovich, and D. Zinnes, *Content Analysis: A Handbook* (Evanston, IL: Northwestern University Press, 1963); Ole Holsti, *Content Analysis for the Social Sciences and Humanities* (Reading, MA: Addison-Wesley Publishing Co., 1969).

7. These rules for conducting systematic content analysis are based on the scientific method employed in various empirical social science approaches. They include (1) the identification of clear and explicitly defined categories for the classification and analysis of data; (2) the

collection of a representative unbiased sample of the data to be analyzed; (3) the selection of the appropriate quantitative technique for analyzing the data sample; and (4) the development of a research design that can be replicated and verified. See especially Ole Holsti, *Content Analysis for the Social Sciences*.

Selltiz, Wrightsman, and Cook, *Research Methods in Social Relations*, p. 392.

For instance, a random sample of Radio Moscow was considered, but was rejected on methodological grounds. This was because the Foreign Broadcast Information Service (FBIS) sampling procedures for reproducing Radio Moscow broadcasts are not based on empirically sound sampling techniques. Consequently, the FBIS sample may be skewed. *New Times* also was considered, but was found too massive a sample for content analysis.

As previously noted, during the first half of the 1960s there were gaps in the weekly appearance of "International Review." To overcome this problem, we analyzed each column paragraph (the unit of analysis is the paragraph), counting each time an opinion about the United States and/or NATO was expressed; summarized the data into twelve-week time periods; and converted the raw data summaries into percentages. This generated 35 data points for trend line analysis.

Those twelve-week periods with publication gaps of several weeks were omitted. This resulted in the subdivision of the 1960–1962 period into two segments (August 1960-April 1961 and November 1961-October 1962). For the same reason, the first data collected for the 1967–1969 period dates from May 1967, as a result of gaps occurring during the early part of the year.

This procedure resulted in 35 twelve-week percentage scores for ten major propaganda themes during the 1960–1962, 1967–1969, and 1976–1979 periods. While our samples are not perfectly equal, in the final analysis they provide a better data base than other available alternatives.

Based on extensive review of the literature cited in previous notes, we believe our research design constitutes an original effort to analyze Soviet foreign propaganda. It is hoped that our approach will serve to stimulate further research on this and related subjects.

For example, "International Review," *Pravda*, October 17, 1960 and November 21, 1960.

"For General and Complete Disarmament," *New Times* (No. 5, 1960), p. 1.

"Total Disarmament: What it Could Mean for the Soviet People," *New Times* (No. 1, 1960), pp. 10–13.

For analyses covering the 1950s and the early 1960s, see Barghoorn, *Soviet Foreign Propaganda*; Clews, *Communist Propaganda Techniques*; Daugherty and Janowitz, ed., *A Psychological Warfare Case-*

book; Alexandra Sulyma, "The Russian Orthodox Church as a Tool
Soviet 'Peace Policy,'" *Ukrainian Quarterly* (March 1958), p
49–57; William Ewer, *Communists on Peace* (London: Batchwo
Press, 1953); Harry Overstreet and Bonaro Overstreet, *The War Call
Peace: Khrushchev's Communism* (New York: Norton, 1961); a
Peter Viereck, "The Trojan Dove," *Russian Review* (January 1953), p
3–15.

16. Barghoorn, *Soviet Foreign Propaganda*, p. 86.

17. See Barghoorn, *Soviet Foreign Propaganda*; and Labin, *The Techniq
of Soviet Propaganda*.

18. For an interesting discussion, see *No Substitute For Peace* (Freder
ton, New Brunswick: Centre for Conflict Studies, University of N
Brunswick, 1982), pp. 5–8.

19. *Ibid.*, p. 7. For a current Soviet statement see Y. Zakharov, "The Wo
Revolutionary Process and Peaceful Coexistence," *Internation
Affairs* (No. 4, 1978).

20. Barghoorn, *Soviet Foreign Propaganda*.

21. "International Review," *Pravda*, August 15, 1960.

22. "Pentagon to Resume Nuclear Testing," *New Times* (No. 2, 196
pp. 3–5; "The Big Hole Theory," *New Times* (No. 6, 1960), pp. 9–
"They Thrive on Provocation and Blood," *New Times* (No. 23, 196
pp. 6–10; "American Provocative Act Against the Soviet Union," *N
Times* (No. 20, 1960), pp. 33–40; and "Secrets of the First Ator
War," *New Times* (No. 29, 1961), pp. 30–31.

23. "What's Happening at the Test-Ban," *New Times* (No. 16, 196
pp. 14–16.

24. *Ibid*; and "No New Approach," *New Times* (No. 13, 1961), p. 2.

25. "International Review," *Pravda*, January 30, 1962; February 26, 19
and March 12, 1962.

26. "Halt the Drift to War," *New Times* (No. 37, 1961), p. 1.

27. "The Outgoing Year," *New Times* (No. 52, 1961), p. 1.

28. *Ibid.*, p. 2.

29. "Exceptional Measures Needed," *New Times* (No. 8, 1962), pp. 4
and "Vital Necessity," *New Times* (No. 10, 1962), pp. 1–2.

30. "Symbol of Hiroshima," *New Times* (No. 29, 1961), pp. 25–31.

31. "Acceptable Nuclear War—The Latest US Theory," *New Times* (
12, 1962), p. 5.

32. *Ibid.*, p. 6.

33. "World Without Weapons," *New Times* (No. 12, 1962), pp. 1–2.

34. In 1962, *New Times* carried a four-part series on the history of the So
disarmament effort beginning with the 1922 Genoa Conference.
"Reminiscences of the 1922 Genoa Conference," *New Times* (
15–18, 1962).

35. "Crime in Space," *New Times* (No. 25, 1962), pp. 9–11; and "Den
tarize Outer Space," *New Times* (No. 26, 1962), p. 6.

36. "Humane Weapons Theory," *New Times* (No. 40, 1962), pp. 13–1

37. "Meaning of the US Disarmament Plan," *New Times* (No. 20, 1962), pp. 30–31.

38. "America's Nuclear Napoleon," *New Times* (No. 27, 1962), pp. 3–4.

39. On Cuba, see "International Review," *Pravda*, September 20, 1960; October 24, 1960; March 6, 1961; September 7, 1962; and October 15, 1962. With respect to Laos, see "International Review," *Pravda*, September 20, 1960; March 6, 1961; and May 24, 1961. Commentary on Berlin includes "International Review," *Pravda*, July 23, 1962; August 27, 1962; and October 15, 1962.

40. "Pentagon Over South Vietnam," *New Times* (No. 30, 1960), pp. 16–17.

41. The four Burchett articles are "On the Border of South Vietnam," *New Times* (No. 23, 1962), pp. 27–30; "South Vietnam: War Against Trees," *New Times* (No. 25, 1962), pp. 24–26; "South Vietnam's Liberation Front," *New Times* (No. 26, 1962), pp. 7–11; and "Report from Hanoi," *New Times* (No. 33, 1962), pp. 14–16.

42. "South Vietnam: War Against Trees," pp. 24–26.

43. *Ibid.*, p. 24.

44. Clews, *Communist Propaganda Techniques*, pp. 146–147. See also John Clews, *The Communists' New Weapon—Germ Warfare* (London: Lincolns Praeger, 1953).

45. "Globke, Eichmann, and Others," *New Times* (No. 42, 1962), p. 14.

46. Other cases received similar coverage, including those of Oberlander and Foertsch. See "Oberlander Case: New Developments," *New Times* (No. 16, 1960), pp. 8–9; and "Career of General Foertsch," *New Times* (No. 6, 1961), pp. 5–11.

47. "German Revanchism and European Peace," *New Times* (No. 19, 1960), p. 12. See also "Father of the Bundeswehr," *New Times* (No. 3, 1960), p. 2; and "International Review," *Pravda*, August 29, 1960 and September 5, 1960.

48. "German Revanchism and European Peace," p. 14.

49. "Father of the Bundeswehr," p. 2. See also "Wolf Without Sheep's Clothing," *New Times* (No. 19, 1961), pp. 28–30.

50. "Right to Self-Determination or Right to Revanche," *New Times* (No. 24, 1960), p. 10.

51. "Bundeswehr—The Nuclear Phase," *New Times* (No. 50, 1961), pp. 10–12.

52. "Bonn Over NATO," *New Times* (No. 31, 1960), p. 9.

53. "The Brown Hand," *New Times* (No. 8, 1960), pp. 10–13.

54. "International Review," *Pravda*, August 29, 1960; April 10, 1961; and November 27, 1961.

55. "International Review," *Pravda*, July 23, 1962.

56. "Washington's European Policy," *New Times* (No. 21, 1961), pp. 11–12; "Europe's Six and Seven and America's Ace," *New Times* (No. 14, 1961), pp. 4–7; "Britain and Kennedy," *New Times* (No. 36, 1961), pp. 14–17; "The NATO Arms-Drive Mechanism," *New Times*

(No. 10, 1962), pp. 4–7; "NATO's Trojan Horse in Northern Europe," *New Times* (No. 19, 1962), pp. 19–22; and "The NATO Military Mechanism," *New Times* (No. 44, 1962), pp. 16–19.

57. "Total Espionage—Some Secrets of Allen Dulles Organization," *New Times* (No. 33, 1960), pp. 10–13; "US Espionage: The Techniques," *New Times* (No. 34, 1960), pp. 13–15; "Plaintive Senator," *New Times* (No. 6, 1962), pp. 16–17; "Secret War On Two Fronts," *New Times* (No. 16, 1962), pp. 13–14; and "The Truth About the Peace Corps," *New Times* (No. 40, 1962), pp. 18–19.

58. "Plaintive Senator," p. 16.

59. For example, "The Capitalist Economy in 1962," *New Times* (No. 7, 1962), pp. 4–7; and "The Capitalist Economy in 1961," *New Times* (No. 10, 1961), pp. 5–7.

60. "International Review," *Pravda*, January 15, 1967; September 25, 1967; January 7, 1968; and February 25, 1968. Beginning with the Tet Offensive in January 1968, the coverage intensified.

61. "The Fighting in Vietnam," *New Times* (No. 30, 1967), pp. 13–14. This charge runs counter to the history of the air war in Vietnam. James Thompson argues that during this period there were target restrictions on these and other sites. See Thompson, *Rolling Thunder: Understanding Policy and Program Failure* (Chapel Hill, NC: University of North Carolina Press, 1980). See also Guenter Lewy, *America in Vietnam* (New York: Oxford University Press, 1978).

62. "Up the Down Staircase," *New Times* (No. 33, 1967), pp. 1–3.

63. "Vietnam and Nuremberg," *New Times* (No. 13, 1967), pp. 29–30.

64. "From the Great Society to the War Society," *New Times* (No. 6, 1967), pp. 13–15; and "Napalm Morality," *New Times* (No. 13, 1967), p. 31.

65. "Washington's Asian Strategy," *New Times* (No. 3, 1969), pp. 11–14.

66. "Up the Down Staircase," pp. 1–3.

67. "Vietnam in Flames," *New Times* (No. 6, 1968), pp. 1–2. This is one of the five articles on Vietnam in this issue.

68. "Will There Be Peace in Vietnam," *New Times* (No. 46, 1968), pp. 2–3; "Americans and Vietnam," *New Times* (No. 48, 1968), pp. 19–20; and "The Paris Talks on the War," *New Times* (No. 16, 1969), pp. 16–19.

69. "International Review," *Pravda*, January 7, 1968; February 11, 1968; and March 25, 1968. Also, "Reaping the Whirlwind," *New Times* (No. 21, 1968), pp. 10–11; "American Youth and the Vietnam War," *New Times* (No. 17, 1969), pp. 9–11; and "Massive Vietnam Protest," *New Times* (No. 42, 1969), pp. 6–7.

70. "Washington's Other War," *New Times* (No. 32, 1967), p. 1. See also "International Review," *Pravda*, March 17, 1968 and April 17, 1968.

71. "Washington's Other War," p. 2.

72. "From the Great Society to the War Society." See also "The Negro Ghetto in Revolt," *New Times* (No. 34, 1967), p. 16.

3. "A Sick Society," *New Times* (No. 32, 1967), pp. 1–2.

4. For example, see "International Review," *Pravda*, July 17, 1967; February 25, 1968; and October 25, 1968.

5. "The Forces Behind the Aggressor," *New Times* (No. 25, 1967), p. 5.

6. *Ibid.*, pp. 5–6.

7. "International Review," *Pravda*, July 7, 1968; July 28, 1968; and August 18, 1968.

8. "International Review," *Pravda*, August 21, 1967.

9. "Bundeswehr Over NATO," *New Times* (No. 35, 1967), p. 6. See also "Bonn's Nuclear Plan," *New Times* (No. 31, 1969), pp. 16–17; and "Bonn's CBW Schemes," *New Times* (No. 38, 1969), pp. 10–11.

0. "Behind Revanche," *New Times* (No. 37, 1967), p. 20.

1. "Bonn Pattern for Europe," *New Times* (No. 15, 1969), p. 18.

2. "US Presence and European Society," *New Times* (No. 17, 1967), pp. 5–9.

3. "NATO Balance Sheet," *New Times* (No. 14, 1969), pp. 10–14.

4. "NATO and the Nuclear Threshold," *New Times* (No. 17, 1969), p. 14.

5. "Reanimating NATO," *New Times* (No. 5, 1969), p. 11.

6. See "Disarmament—A Common Responsibility," *New Times* (No. 52, 1968), p. 2.

7. "International Review," *Pravda*, March 23, 1969.

8. "International Review," *Pravda*, December 21, 1969.

9. *Ibid.*

0. "International Review," *Pravda*, August 17, 1969.

1. Adam Ulam, *Dangerous Relations: The Soviet Union in World Politics* (New York: Oxford University Press, 1983), pp. 83–88.

2. *Ibid.*, p. 96.

3. "International Review," *Pravda*, April 22, 1976 and May 13, 1976.

4. "International Review," *Pravda*, March 21, 1976.

5. "International Review," *Pravda*, January 16, 1976.

5. "Detente Requires Cooperation," *New Times* (No. 47, 1976), p. 1.

7. *Ibid.*

8. "Pentagon Opposition," *New Times* (No. 48, 1976), p. 10.

9. "The 39th President Takes Over," *New Times* (No. 4, 1977), p. 9.

00. *Ibid.*

01. "Evolution of US Foreign Policy Thinking," *New Times* (No. 7, 1977), p. 10.

02. "International Review," *Pravda*, June 20, 1976.

03. "International Review," *Pravda*, December 21, 1969.

04. "International Review," *Pravda*, June 20, 1979.

05. "USSR-West Germany: On the Road of Detente and Cooperation," *New Times* (No. 17, 1978), p. 6.

06. *Ibid.*

07. See, for example, "Pentagon Opposition," *New Times* (No. 48, 1976), pp. 10–11.

108. "The 39th President Takes Over," p. 8.
109. *Ibid.*, pp. 8–9.
110. *Ibid.*
111. "That Old Bogey," *New Times* (No. 38, 1976), pp. 14–15.
112. "Death Merchants," *New Times* (No. 47, 1976), pp. 20–22. See also "Pentagon: Arms and Money," *New Times* (No. 40, 1976), pp. 21–24.
113. "Pentagon's Nuclear Strategy," *New Times* (No. 35, 1977), p. 22.
114. "Weapons Cannot Be Humane," *New Times* (No. 31, 1977), p. 8.
115. "Pentagon: Arms and Money," p. 22.
116. *Ibid.*
117. "Brinkmanship Again," *New Times* (No. 7, 1976), p. 21.
118. "NATO Obstructions in Vienna," *New Times* (No. 25, 1977), p. 10.
119. "International Review," *Pravda*, December 11, 1977; December 18 1977; December 25, 1977; January 24, 1978; and February 19, 1978
120. "In the White House or the Pentagon?", *New Times* (No. 28, 1977) p. 1.
121. *Ibid.*
122. "Dangerous Course," *New Times* (No. 27, 1978), p. 12.
123. *Ibid.*, pp. 12–13.
124. *Ibid.*, p. 13.
125. "Military-Industrial Complex: Money, Arms, Power," *New Times* (No. 23, 1978), pp. 23–24.
126. *Ibid.*, p. 26.
127. *Ibid.*
128. *Ibid.*
129. *Documents on Disarmament* (Washington, DC: Arms Control and Disarmament Agency, 1978), pp. 281–282.
130. "International Review," *Pravda*, June 19, 1977; December 18, 1977 December 25, 1977; January 29, 1978; and February 5, 1978. Also "Neutron Bomb: Squaring the Circle," *New Times* (No. 35, 1977), pp 6–8; "The Neutron Peril," *New Times* (No. 1, 1978), pp. 26–27; and "Neutron Maniacs," *New Times* (No. 9, 1978), pp. 14–15. The Soviet charges went so far as to label the neutron weapon a racist weapon that the "imperialists might be tempted to use to put an end to population inflation in the developing world." "Neutron Bomb is a Racist Weapon," *New Times* (No. 18, 1978), p. 15.
131. "N-Bomb Over Europe," *New Times* (No. 36, 1977), p. 13.
132. *Ibid.*
133. "No to the Bomb," *New Times* (No. 36, 1977), pp. 14–15; "Policy and Rhetoric," *New Times* (No. 4, 1978), pp. 10–11; and "Common Sense vs. Neutron Madness," *New Times* (No. 7, 1978), pp. 12–13
134. "International Review," *Pravda*, December 10, 1978.
135. "The Law of Life and the Apostles of Nuclear Death," *New Times* (No. 22, 1979), pp. 8–9.

136. "The Difficult Road to Ratification," *New Times* (No. 33, 1979), p. 11.

137. "Does NATO Need the Euromissiles?", *New Times* (No. 44, 1979), pp. 4–5; and "Pentagon, NATO, and Euromissiles," *New Times* (No. 9, 1979), pp. 8–9. Also, "International Review," *Pravda*, December 2, 1979; December 16, 1979; and December 23, 1979.

138. "NATO: Myths and the Reality," *New Times* (No. 14, 1979), pp. 20–30.

139. "International Review," *Pravda*, August 12, 1979.

140. *Ibid.*

141. *Ibid.*

142. "Does NATO Need Euromissiles?", p. 5.

143. "The NATO Missile Frenzy," *New Times* (No. 48, 1979), pp. 4–5; and "Hegemonist Geopolitical Thinking," *New Times* (No. 50, 1979), pp. 18–19.

144. "NATO: Suicidal Risk," *New Times* (No. 52, 1979), p. 7.

145. See, for example, "International Review," *Pravda*, February 8, 1976; April 4, 1976; May 30, 1976; and August 26, 1979.

146. "CIA Subversion in Angola," *New Times* (No. 3, 1976), pp. 10–11; "The Battle for Angola," *New Times* (No. 6, 1976), pp. 8–9; "Imperialism Against Africa," *New Times* (No. 28, 1978), pp. 18–30; "Neo-Colonial Strategem in Africa," *New Times* (No. 35, 1978), pp. 18–19; and "International Review," *Pravda*, August 26, 1979.

147. The coverage during the latter part of 1978 and the early part of 1979 was quite extensive. For selected examples, see "Iran—Deep Crisis," *New Times* (No. 39, 1978), pp. 10–11; "Iran: Crisis Pitch," *New Times* (No. 51, 1978), pp. 10–11; "Iran—At the Crossroads," *New Times* (No. 2, 1979), pp. 8–9; and "Iran—The People's Wrath," *New Times* (No. 6, 1979), pp. 12–13.

148. "Imperialist Design in the Horn of Africa," *New Times* (No. 7, 1978), pp. 4–5.

149. This was not a new theme, as noted in our prior analysis. However, the scope of the attack against the CIA appears to have intensified during the 1976–1979 period.

150. "On the Trail of a President's Killers," *New Times* (No. 2, 1977), pp. 26–30.

151. *Ibid.*

152. "On the Trail of a President's Killers," *New Times* (No. 3, 1977), p. 30.

153. "Langely Silhouettes," *New Times* (Nos. 43, 46, and 50, 1979).

154. *Ibid.* (No. 43, 1979), p. 26.

155. *Ibid.*

156. *Ibid.*

CHAPTER 4

1. Based on confidential Comintern documents first published in 1924 in German by the German Trade Union Federation (ADGB), under the title "The Third Column of Communist Policy—IAH (International Worker's Aid)." Quoted in English in *Labour Magazine* (December 1924). The quotations were authenticated by Willi Munzenberg's widow, Babette Gross, in her book entitled *Willi Munzenberg—A Political Biography* (Lansing, MI: Michigan State University Press, 1974), pp. 121 and 133.

2. *Fourth Congress of the Communist International*, Abridged Report of Meetings Held at Petrograd and Moscow, November 7-December 3, 1922 (London: Communist Party of Great Britain), p. 53.

3. *Seventh Congress of the Communist International*, Abridged Stenographic Report of Proceedings, July-August 1935 (Moscow: Foreign Languages Publishing House, 1939), p. 489.

4. As previously explained, in 1957 the International Department of the CPSU's Central Committee took over the responsibility for coordinating and directing the international front organizations.

5. *Meeting of the Information Bureau of Communist Parties—in Hungary in the Latter Half of November 1949*, published by the journal *For a Lasting Peace, For a People's Democracy* (The Cominform organ), printed in the USSR, 1950, p. 48. Reprinted by the Communist Party of the USA under the title *Working Class Unity for Peace* (New York: New Century Publishers, 1950).

6. *Ibid.*, p. 49.

7. *Ibid.*, p. 49.

8. See Roy Godson, *Labor in Soviet Global Strategy* (New York: Crane, Russak and Co., [1984]).

9. *Documents of the Ninth Congress of the Communist Party of India, 1971* (New Delhi: Communist Party Publications, 1972), p. 414.

10. Romesh Chandra, "Postponing or Eliminating the Threat of War," *World Marxist Review* (January 1981), pp. 31–35.

11. *Ibid.*, p. 35.

12. *The World Peace Council: What It Is and What It Does* (Helsinki: World Peace Council, 1978).

13. *Ibid.* During the 1980–1983 period, the membership of these WPC bodies remained relatively the same. See *World Peace Council List of Members, 1980–1983* (Helsinki: World Peace Council, 1982). See also the data and analysis in Wallace H. Spaulding, "The Communist Movement and Its Allies," in Ralph M. Goldman, ed., *Transnational Parties* (Lanham, MD: University Press of America, 1983).

14. US Congress, House, Permanent Select Committee on Intelligence "Soviet Active Measures," 97th Congress, 2nd Session (Washington DC: GPO, 1982), pp. 198–236.

5. US Congress, House, *Congressional Record*, 97th Cong. 2nd Sess., 1983, P.H.-1791. *(FBI Intelligence Division Report on Soviet Active Measures Relating to the US Peace Movement.)*

6. US Congress, House, Permanent Select Committee on Intelligence, "Soviet Active Measures," p. 203.

7. *Party Organizer*, Vol. XVI (Nos. 4, 5, 6, 1982), pp. 48–49. An article by Myerson discusses the work of the CPUSA and the US Peace Council which was directed at the 1982 UN Special Session on Disarmament.

8. *FBI Intelligence Division Report on Soviet Active Measures.*

9. *Ibid.*

0. *Ibid.*

1. Ronald Radosh, "The Peace Council and Peace," *New Republic* (January 31, 1983), p. 16.

2. *FBI Intelligence Division Report on Soviet Active Measures.*

3. US Congress, House, Permanent Select Committee on Intelligence, "Soviet Active Measures," p. 298.

4. *Party Organizer*, Vol. XVI (No. 1, 1982), p. 31.

5. *The World Peace Council: What It Is and What It Does.*

6. US Congress, House, Permanent Select Committee on Intelligence, "Soviet Covert Action (The Forgery Offensive)," 96th Congress, 2nd Session (Washington DC: GPO, 1980), p. 79.

7. Letter to the editor from Ruth Tosek, *New Statesman* (October 17, 1980), p. 22.

8. For information on International Department officials serving as WPC officers and attending WPC meetings, see the WPC publications previously cited. On the subject of ID control of WPC President Romesh Chandra and the WPC Secretariat, see US Congress, House, Permanent Select Committee on Intelligence, "The CIA and the Media," 95th Congress, 1st and 2nd Sessions (Washington, DC: GPO, April 20, 1978), p. 571. On Soviet control and financing of national Communist parties (particularly the CPUSA) and on KGB involvement, see US Congress, House, Permanent Select Committee on Intelligence, "Soviet Active Measures," pp. 22, 56–57, 70, 165–167, and 202–235.

A number of peace activists who have worked for or with the WPC and other fronts also have maintained that Moscow exerts overwhelming control over these organizations. See, for example, statements by Richard K. Ullman, former Vice President of the Christian Peace Conference, in his *Dilemmas of a Reconciler: Serving the East-West Conflict* (Wallingford, PA: Pendle Hill, 1963); and Jiri Pelikan, former head of the International Union of Students, in his article "The Struggle for Socialism in Czechoslovakia," *New Left Review* (January-February 1972). E.P. Thompson, a British proponent of unilateral nuclear disarmament, also has warned anti-war activists to beware of the WPC. (*The Guardian* [London], February 18, 1981.)

Probably the best single secondary source on ID and KGB manipulation of the WPC and its American and European affiliates is John Barron's *The KGB Today* (New York: Reader's Digest Press, 1983). For a contrary view, see Frank Donner, "But Will They Come?", *The Nation* (November 6, 1982), pp. 456–465.

29. *Meeting of the Information Bureau of Communist Parties*, p. 36.
30. *Ibid.*, p. 53.
31. *In Defense of Peace* (April 1950), p. 2.
32. World Peace Movement, *Resolutions and Documents* (n.p.: Secretariat of the World Council of Peace, 1955), p. 47.
33. *World Youth* (July 1950), p. 2.
34. Nikolai Mikhailov, *We Live to Bring Peace* (Moscow: Novosti Press Agency, [circa late 1960s]), p. 15. An editorial in the April 1950 issue of *World Youth*, the WFDY magazine, revealed that "the Soviet people, led by Stalin, is [sic] now at the head of the camp of peace and democracy."
35. *Meeting of the Information Bureau of Communist Parties*, p. 54.
36. *Ibid.* In what must be characterized as a revealing explanation of the Communist "peace offensive," Maurice Thorez, head of the French Communist Party, and Palmiro Togliatti, head of the Italian Communist Party, announced that they would welcome the Soviet army when it entered their countries, "in its battle against the aggressor." See *For a Lasting Peace, For a People's Democracy* (March 1 and 15, 1949).
37. *Schwarzbuch Uber den Bakterienkrieg* (Blackbook on Germ Warfare) (Vienna: Osterreichischen Friedensrat [Austrian Peace Council], June 1952), p. 2.
38. *World Peace Movement Resolutions and Documents*, pp. 102–103.
39. *World Student News* (No. 11, 1952), p. 5.
40. *World Youth* (July, 1952), p. 3.
41. Louis Saillant, *The WFTU and the Tasks of the Trade Union Movement*, Report to the Fifth Congress of the WFTU, Moscow, December 4–16, 1961 (London: WFTU Publications Ltd., 1961), pp. 20–21.
42. *Assembly of the World Peace Council, Documents*, Budapest, May 13–166, 1971 (Helsinki: World Peace Council, 1971), p. 54.
43. *World Student News* (Nos. 11–12, 1964), p. 8.
44. *8th International Union of Students Congress, Resolutions* (Sofia, Bulgaria: November 28-December 10, 1964), p. 8.
45. See, for example, *Documentary Record, WFDY Executive Committee Meeting*, Moscow, November 16–18, 1972 (Budapest: WFDY, 1972), p. 72.
46. *Assembly of the World Peace Council, Documents*, Budapest, May 13–16, 1971, p. 43.
47. Mimeographed documents appended to letter of Bertil Svahnstrom, chairman of the International Liaison Committee of the Stockholm Conference on Vietnam, May 23, 1969.

48. *World Peace Council Information Letter #2* of the Stockholm Conference (Stockholm: World Peace Council, May 7, 1970), p. 5.
49. *Ibid.*
50. *Ibid.*
51. *Neutron Bombs No!* (Helsinki: World Peace Council, September 1977), pp. 6–7.
52. *Ibid.*, p. 7.
53. *Ibid.*, pp. 39–40.
54. *Ibid.*, pp. 50 and 53.
55. *New Perspectives* (March 1978), p. 6.
56. *World Peace Council and Disarmament* (Helsinki: World Peace Council, May 27, 1978), pp. 1, 7, and 8.
57. *World Peace Council and Disarmament* (Helsinki: World Peace Council, June 8, 1978), p. 4.
58. *Stoppt die Neutronen Bombe* (Stop the Neutron Bomb), published by SEW-Hochschulgruppe (Socialist Unity Party West Berlin, High School Group), circa mid-1978.
59. Moscow TASS International Service in Russia, August 10, 1981, translated in *FBIS Daily Report*, Soviet Union, Vol. III (August 11, 1981), p. AA1.
60. Moscow TASS, August 13, 1981, translated in *FBIS Daily Report*, Soviet Union, Vol. III (August 14, 1981), p. AA4.
61. Moscow Domestic Service in Russian, August 14, 1981, translated in *FBIS Daily Report*, Soviet Union, Vol. III (August 17, 1981), p. CC7.
62. Moscow TASS in English, *FBIS Daily Report*, Soviet Union, Vol. III (August 19, 1981), p. AA3.
63. *Peace Courier* (September 1981), p. 1.
64. *Pravda*, January 28, 1982, p. 1. Translated in *FBIS Daily Report*, Soviet Union, Vol. III (February 2, 1981), p. CC1.
65. *International Trade Union Round Table, Detente-Conversion-Disarmament* (Prague: WFTU, 1981), p. 6.
66. *Ibid.*, p. 11.
67. World Federation of Democratic Youth, *Youth Disarmament—Facts, Arguments, Information* (Budapest: WFDY, 1982).
68. *Peace Courier* (August 1975), p. 1.
69. *Rights of the Palestinian People—Key to Peace in the Middle East*, International Conference of Solidarity with the Palestinian People, Basle, Switzerland, May 4–6, 1979 (Helsinki: World Peace Council, May 1979), pp. 11–13.
70. Havana Domestic Service in Spanish, April 21, 1981, translated in *FBIS Daily Report*, Latin America, Vol. VI (April 22, 1981), p. 2.
71. See *Paris Match* (July 11, 1980); and the *Daily Telegraph*, July 14, 1980. See also US Congress, House, Permanent Select Committee on Intelligence, "Soviet Active Measures," pp. 42–43.
72. These include *Realite, Liberation, France-Observateur, L'Evenement,*

Le Nouvel Observateur, Option, and *Vie Ouvrier.*

73. *Synthesis* was published bimonthly from July 1976 until the arrest of Pathe in July 1979—a period of almost exactly three years. The length of the newsletter averaged eight legal-size pages. Each issue contained three to five articles on political, economic, military, and scientific subjects. The content and themes of these articles are analyzed later in this study.
74. *Paris Match* (July 11, 1980).
75. *Synthesis* (April 20, 1977).
76. *Ibid.* (February 20, 1978).
77. *Ibid.* (August 20, 1977 and February 20, 1978).
78. *Ibid.* (January 5, 1978).
79. *Ibid.* (December 5, 1976).
80. *Ibid.* (May 20, 1977).
81. *Ibid.* (February 5, 1979).
82. *Ibid.* (January 5, 1978).
83. *Ibid.* (January 20, 1979).
84. *Ibid.* (March 5, 1977).
85. *Ibid.* (April 20, 1977 and April 20, 1978).
86. *Ibid.* (March 5, 1978).
87. *Ibid.* (March 5, 1977).
88. *Ibid.* (September 20, 1977).
89. *Ibid.* (April 5, 1979).
90. *Ibid.* (June 5, 1977).
91. *Ibid.* (March 20, 1979).
92. *Ibid.* (November 5, 1976 and November 20, 1977).
93. *Ibid.* (April 5, 1977).
94. *Ibid.* (March 20, 1978).
95. *Ibid.*
96. *Ibid.* (March 20, 1979).
97. *Ibid.* (April 5, 1977).
98. *Ibid.* (June 5, 1977).
99. *Ibid.*
100. *Ibid.* (September 5, 1976).
101. *Ibid.* (June 20, 1978).
102. *Ibid.*
103. *Ibid.* (February 20, 1978).
104. *Ibid.* (May 20, 1977).
105. *Ibid.* (March 5, 1979).
106. *Ibid.* (February 20, 1978).
107. *Ibid.* (September 5, 1977).
108. *Ibid.* (January 20, 1979).
109. *Ibid.* (February 5, 1979 and February 20, 1979).
110. *Ibid.* (March 20, 1979).
111. *Ibid.* (March 5, 1979).
112. *Ibid.* (December 20, 1978).

113. *Ibid.* (March 20, 1978).
114. *Ibid.* (November 5, 1977).
115. *Ibid.* (May 20, 1978).
116. *Ibid.*
117. *Ibid.* (June 5, 1978).
118. *Ibid.* (May 5, 1978).
119. *Ibid.* (July 20, 1978). See also *Ibid.* (November 5, 1978).
120. *Ibid.* (November 5, 1978).
121. *Ibid.*
122. *Ibid.* See also *Ibid.* (November 5, 1977).
123. Geoffrey Bailey, *The Conspirators* (New York: Harper, 1960), p. 306.
124. The Soviet forgeries reviewed in this study are drawn from US Congress, Senate, Committee on the Judiciary Subcommittee to Investigate the Administration of the Internal Security Act, "Communist Forgeries," 87th Congress, 1st Session (Washington, DC: GPO, 1961); US Congress, House, Permanent Select Committee on Intelligence, "Soviet Covert Action (The Forgery Offensive)"; and US Congress, House, Permanent Select Committee on Intelligence, "Soviet Active Measures."
125. Ladislav Bittman, "Soviet Bloc 'Disinformation' and other 'Active Measures,'" in Robert L. Pfaltzgraff, Uri Ra'anan, and Warren Milberg, ed., *Intelligence Policy and National Security* (Hamden, CT: Archon Books, 1982), p. 217. Also see Jan Sejna, *We Will Bury You* (London: Sidgwick and Jackson, 1982), for a discussion by a former Czech General about how political warfare fits into overall Soviet strategic planning.
126. US Congress, Senate, Committee on the Judiciary Subcommittee to Investigate the Administration of the Internal Security Act, "Communist Forgeries."
127. *Ibid.*, p. 22.
128. *Ibid.*, p. 56.
129. *Ibid.*, p. 24.
130. An excerpt from one of these letters reads: "I am an American pilot who lost a friend flying over Eastern Germany. I intend to get my revenge by dropping an atomic bomb on Soviet territory." *Ibid.*, p. 92.
131. *Ibid.*, pp. 12–13.
132. *Ibid.*, p. 44.
133. *Ibid.*, pp. 12, 13, 18, and 31.
134. *Ibid.*, pp. 7 and 9.
135. *Ibid.*, pp. 20 and 30.
136. US Congress, House, Permanent Select Committee on Intelligence, "Soviet Active Measures," p. 77.
137. *Ibid.*, p. 78.
138. *Ibid.*, pp. 78–79.
139. *Ibid.*, p. 79.
140. *Ibid.*, p. 83.

141. *Ibid.*, p. 84.
142. *Ibid.*, p. 91.
143. US Congress, House, Permanent Select Committee on Intelligence, "Soviet Covert Action (The Forgery Offensive)," p. 137.
144. US Congress, House, Permanent Select Committee on Intelligence, "Soviet Active Measures," pp. 122–124.
145. US Congress, House, Permanent Select Committee on Intelligence, "Soviet Covert Action (The Forgery Offensive)," p. 133.
146. *Ibid.*, p. 122.
147. *Ibid.*, pp. 122–123.
148. US Congress, House, Permanent Select Committee on Intelligence, "Soviet Active Measures," pp. 119–121.
149. *Ibid.*, p. 95.
150. In 1967, for example, there appeared a doctored US State Department airgram to members of several West European governments instructing the recipients to collect information on ways to bribe European officials, and to develop other ways to damage or eliminate foreign trade competition. The original document simply contained worldwide economic information for the Fiscal Year 1975. US Congress, House, Permanent Select Committee on Intelligence, "Soviet Covert Action (The Forgery Offensive)," p. 102.
151. *Ibid.*, pp. 147 and 153–156.
152. *Ibid.*, p. 125; and US Congress, House, Permanent Select Committee on Intelligence, "Soviet Active Measures," pp. 111–119 and 133–135.
153. *Ibid.*, pp. 89–90.
154. *Ibid.*, pp. 93–94. Another example was a fabricated US-Swedish mailgram which allegedly revealed a US-Swedish agreement providing for American use of Swedish facilities at Karlskrona for reconnaissance purposes. One purpose of the mailgram may have been to distract world attention from the recent violation of Swedish territorial waters by a nuclear-armed Soviet submarine. *Ibid.*, pp. 105–110.
155. US Congress, House, Permanent Select Committee on Intelligence, "Soviet Covert Action (The Forgery Offensive)," pp. 86–101.

CHAPTER 5

1. See Ladislav Bittman's book *The Deception Game* (Syracuse, NY Syracuse University Research Corp., 1972), and his Congressional testimony in US Congress, House, Permanent Select Committee on Intelligence, "Soviet Covert Action (The Forgery Offensive)," 96th Congress, 2nd Session (Washington, DC: GPO, 1980), pp. 34–58. Levchenko's Congressional statement is in US Congress, House, Per-

manent Select Committee on Intelligence, "Soviet Active Measures," 97th Congress, 2nd Session (Washington, DC: GPO, 1982), pp. 138–169.
2. For a thorough discussion of Operation Neptune, see Bittman, *The Deception Game*, Chapter 2.

INDEX

ABOUT THE AUTHORS

Roy Godson is Associate Professor of Government at Georgetown University, specializing in international relations and intelligence studies. He is the author of numerous books and articles on national security and statecraft, and is the editor of the multi-volume series *Intelligence Requirements for the 1980s*.

Richard H. Shultz currently is Associate Professor of International Politics at the Fletcher School of Law and Diplomacy where he teaches international security affairs. He is on leave from Catholic University. He has published numerous articles and is the co-author of *Lessons from an Unconventional War*.

True accounts of Vietnam.

From the men who saw it all.
Did it all. And lived to tell it all.